NTC's PRACTICE TESTS FOR THE

TOEFL®

TEST OF ENGLISH AS A FOREIGN LANGUAGE

Second Edition

Milada Broukal • **Enid Nolan-Woods**

National Textbook Company
a division of NTC/CONTEMPORARY PUBLISHING COMPANY
Lincolnwood, Illinois USA

Cover design: Nick Panos

ISBN: 0-8442-0495-1

Published by National Textbook Company,
a division of NTC/Contemporary Publishing Company,
4255 West Touhy Avenue,
Lincolnwood (Chicago), Illinois 60646-1975 U.S.A.
Originally published by Macmillan Publishers Ltd.

TOEFL test directions and TWE scoring guidelines are reprinted by permission
of Educational Testing Service, the copyright owner. However, the test
questions and other testing information are provided in their entirety
by National Textbook Company. No endorsement of this publication by
Educational Testing Service should be inferred.

4 5 6 7 8 9 0 VLP VLP 0 5

Contents

Introduction

Who is this book for?

It is for all students whose native language is not English and who wish to take the TOEFL (Test of English as a Foreign Language).

What is TOEFL?

The TOEFL is a test which measures your ability to use the English language and demonstrates your level of efficiency. The test is divided into three sections, each section testing an important language skill.

Section 1: Listening Comprehension

This section tests your ability to understand spoken North American English. All of the questions in this section are recorded on a tape which you will listen to.
    Part A: Conversations
    Part B: Longer conversations
    Part C: Talks
    Section total: 35 minutes   50 questions

Section 2: Structure and Written Expression

This section measures your ability to recognize language that is appropriate for standard written English. Your knowledge of English structures and grammar, use and usage, word order, and sentence structure will all be tested.
    First part: Incomplete sentences
    Second part: Incorrect words and phrases
    Section total: 25 minutes   40 questions

Section 3: Reading Comprehension

This section measures your ability to understand different kinds of reading material, as well as testing your ability to understand the meaning and use of words.
    Total: 55 minutes   50 questions

    Overall total: 1 hour 55 minutes   140 questions

In addition to the TOEFL, it is also possible to take the Test of Written English (TWE) which measures your ability to write clearly in standard English.

Test of Written English (TWE)

Written essay: 30 minutes   approximately 200-300 words

How can I register for the TOEFL?

The TOEFL is administered in the United States and abroad at officially designated Test Centers. Names and locations of these centers, and dates of administration, are found in the Bulletin of Information, which you can obtain free from the Educational Testing Service (ETS) at the following address: TOEFL, P.O. Box 6151, Princeton, NJ 08541-6151, USA.

You may take the TOEFL as many times as you wish, but if it is more than two years since you last took the test, then your score is no longer valid, and you must retake the TOEFL before entering an application to a college or university. A Handbook for Applicants is also available free of charge from ETS to students who have registered to take the TOEFL.

How can this book help me pass the TOEFL?

This book contains all the practice test material that you will need to pass the TOEFL. Five complete tests, with almost exactly the same instructions, type of material, layout, and timing as in the TOEFL are included for your practice. In addition, there are complete answer keys to all the questions, complete tapescripts of all the material in the Listening Comprehension sections, and a sample answer sheet for you to study. It is suggested that you keep strictly to the timing given when you practice these tests, and on *no account* should you look at the answers or tapescripts until you have completed and scored a test.

We advise you to aim for a score of 500 as this is generally the lowest score accepted by a good college or university in the United States. Some colleges and universities require 550+ for graduate or Arts courses and any score below 450 is not considered for admission without an intensive ESL program.

We hope you enjoy using this book and feel sure that if you work through it steadily, you will obtain the necessary score to continue your studies in an English-speaking college or university.

Milada L. Broukal
1996
Los Angeles, U.S.A.

Enid M. Nolan-Woods
1996
London, England

PRACTICE TEST 1

SECTION 1
LISTENING COMPREHENSION

In this section of the test, you will have an opportunity to demonstrate your ability to understand conversations and talks in English. In this section, there are answers to all the questions based on the information heard.

Part A

Directions: In Part A, you will hear short conversations between two people. At the end of each conversation, you will hear a question about the conversation. The conversation and question will not be repeated. Therefore, you must listen carefully to understand what each speaker says. After you hear a question, read the four possible answers in your test book and choose the best answer to the question you heard. Then, on your answer sheet, find the number of the question and fill in the space that corresponds to the letter of the answer you have chosen.

Listen to an example on the recording:

Man: **What seems to be the problem, ma'am?**
Woman: **Well, the light switch is broken and a plug needs repairing.**
Question: **What kind of work does the man probably do?**

In your book you will read: (A) He's a carpenter.
                            (B) He's a plumber.
                            (C) He's an electrician.
                            (D) He's an engineer.

From the conversation, you learn that the light switch is broken and a plug needs repairing. The best answer to the question, "What kind of work does the man probably do?" is *He's an electrician*. Therefore, the correct choice is (C).

Sample Answer
Ⓐ Ⓑ ● Ⓓ

1. (A) In a hospital.
    (B) At a museum.
    (C) In a supermarket.
    (D) At a church.

2. (A) Her central heating system needs checking.
    (B) She would like to pay the man.
    (C) Part of her car requires attention.
    (D) She wants to look at some hoods.

3. (A) He called up his sister.
    (B) He went to San Francisco.
    (C) He visited his sister.
    (D) He stayed at home.

4. (A) She hasn't been speeding.
    (B) She doesn't have her driving license in the car.
    (C) Her car is unlicensed.
    (D) She wants to get her car registered.

5. (A) Mr. Phillips will not be in this office at all this week.
    (B) He will be here on Tuesday only.
    (C) He'll be here on Monday, Wednesday and Friday.
    (D) He'll be at this office on Tuesday and Thursday.

GO ON TO THE NEXT PAGE ➤

6. (A) Leave the restaurant without paying.
   (B) Give the waiter a small tip.
   (C) Complain about the food.
   (D) Eat some more shrimps.

7. (A) He didn't have enough money to go to the concert.
   (B) He arrived too late to hear the concert.
   (C) He altered his plans suddenly.
   (D) He plans to go to the concert tonight instead.

8. (A) It isn't big enough.
   (B) There are only two bedrooms.
   (C) It's too noisy.
   (D) The air conditioning causes a problem.

9. (A) Take her mother to a show.
   (B) Go to the basketball game.
   (C) Buy some tickets for the basketball game.
   (D) Go to a show with her sister.

10. (A) Dinner is going to be late.
    (B) The ice cream won't be set in time for dinner.
    (C) There isn't enough ice cream for dinner.
    (D) The ice cream will just about go around at dinner.

11. (A) Manicurist.
    (B) Store clerk.
    (C) Supermarket manager.
    (D) Waitress.

12. (A) The woman likes to wear gloves.
    (B) She has beautiful eyes.
    (C) The dress suits her very well.
    (D) Her eyes and gloves are the same color.

13. (A) Go to the dance alone.
    (B) Take someone else to the dance.
    (C) Stand in line for tickets to the dance.
    (D) Not go to the dance at all.

14. (A) Bank manager and customer.
    (B) Store clerk and buyer.
    (C) College student and professor.
    (D) Assembly worker and supervisor.

15. (A) Go to a fast-food place with the man.
    (B) Eat after her class.
    (C) Join some friends for a quick meal.
    (D) Get to her class early.

16. (A) He didn't want to go to the ballet.
    (B) He was looking forward to seeing the ballet.
    (C) He had another date for the evening.
    (D) He was a convincing young man.

17. (A) Leon has already left without them.
    (B) He thinks the woman should call Leon.
    (C) Leon already knows they're going to be late.
    (D) Leon probably won't be in the house to receive the call.

18. (A) She's getting old.
    (B) She's learning something new about philosophy every day.
    (C) It's going to take her a long time to master philosophy.
    (D) She loves her philosophy class so much, she could take it forever.

19. (A) What kind of questions will be on the test.
    (B) Where Martha got her information.
    (C) How Martha did on the test.
    (D) Why Martha would talk about the test.

20. (A) He doesn't see Peter very often.
    (B) He agrees that Peter is good at fixing cars.
    (C) He doesn't think Peter is a good mechanic.
    (D) He watched Peter fix his car once.

GO ON TO THE NEXT PAGE

21. (A) Actor and director.
    (B) Salesman and buyer.
    (C) Repairperson and customer.
    (D) Ticket seller and concert goer.

22. (A) He'd like to own a bank.
    (B) He wishes his niece knew how to drive.
    (C) He'd like to buy the car for himself.
    (D) He can't afford to buy the car.

23. (A) What reason the woman has for driving all the way to Pasadena.
    (B) Why the woman would rather be at the parade than watch it on TV.
    (C) How the woman plans to watch the Rose Bowl parade.
    (D) When the woman expects to go to the parade.

24. (A) Evelyn took her test in another town.
    (B) Evelyn took her test before the other students.
    (C) Evelyn isn't taking Asian history.
    (D) Evelyn wanted to be the first student out of town.

25. (A) She decided not to send an application to Stanford.
    (B) She had already applied to Stanford.
    (C) Her grades weren't good enough for Stanford.
    (D) After all her hard work, she couldn't go to Stanford.

26. (A) She'd be happy to run the potter's wheel.
    (B) She doesn't know how to work the potter's wheel.
    (C) She'd rather check the oven.
    (D) She's too busy to help the man.

27. (A) She and Rene exercised a lot before the test.
    (B) She had to drive back to Rene's several times to help him study.
    (C) She did everything she could to help Rene prepare for his test.
    (D) She taught Rene how to do back-flips to get ready for his test.

28. (A) That the woman should buy a new model at a later time.
    (B) That the woman should buy the latest model now.
    (C) That the woman's computer will be good until June.
    (D) That the woman should buy a computer like the model he has.

29. (A) She doesn't like fashion shows.
    (B) She's already made other plans for Saturday.
    (C) She hopes to meet the man at the show.
    (D) She loves going to museums on Saturday.

30. (A) He knew every candidate he voted for.
    (B) He was voting at the same time as the woman.
    (C) He was disappointed because he didn't win the election.
    (D) He was unhappy because his candidates weren't elected.

GO ON TO THE NEXT PAGE

Part B

Directions: In this part, you will hear longer conversations. After each conversation, you will be asked several questions. You will hear the conversations and the questions about them only one time. They will not be repeated. Therefore, you must listen carefully to understand what each speaker says.

After you hear a question, read the four possible answers in your test book and choose which one is the best answer to the question you heard. Then, on your answer sheet, find the number of the question and fill in the space that corresponds to the letter of the answer you have chosen.

Remember, you should not take notes or write on your test paper.

31. (A) Why Melissa is late.
    (B) What they need for their presentation.
    (C) How Mr. Mahoney can help them with his clipper ship.
    (D) What would happen if they didn't do their presentation.

32. (A) In a library.
    (B) In a laboratory.
    (C) In an antique shop.
    (D) In a book and map store.

33. (A) She needs help.
    (B) She's rude.
    (C) She's always busy.
    (D) She's nice.

34. (A) Chemistry.
    (B) Art History.
    (C) World History.
    (D) American Literature.

35. (A) To register for courses.
    (B) To inquire about registering for certain courses.
    (C) To confirm a prior registration for courses.
    (D) To drop a course.

36. (A) After the person's sociology class.
    (B) At the end of the semester.
    (C) Before the start of the semester.
    (D) The evening before classes start.

37. (A) Patient and cordial.
    (B) Irritated but polite.
    (C) Confused and angry.
    (D) Disinterested

38. (A) Sociology.
    (B) Social Studies.
    (C) Policy Studies.
    (D) Managerial Studies.

GO ON TO THE NEXT PAGE

1 • 1 • 1 • 1 • 1 • 1 • 1

Part C

<u>Directions</u>: In this part, you will hear various talks. After each talk, you will be asked several questions. The talks and questions will not be repeated. They will not be written out for you. Therefore, you must listen carefully to understand what the speaker says.

After you hear a question, read the four possible answers in your test book and choose which one is the best answer to the question you heard. Then, on your answer sheet, find the number of the question and fill in the space that corresponds to the letter of the answer you have chosen.

Listen to this sample talk.

You will hear: **The National Health Research Center, perhaps more than any other organization, will directly affect the lives of millions of Americans every day. The Health Research Center volunteers will work all over the United States to provide information on diet and lifestyles. The bulk of the foundation's time will be spent conducting seminars and distributing pamphlets on how to prevent major illness and increase longevity. A free long-distance 800 number is available for anyone with health-related questions.**

Now listen to the following question.

What is the speaker's purpose?

You will read: (A) To get you to join the foundation.
(B) To inform you of the existence of the Health Research Center.
(C) To persuade you to give a donation to the foundation.
(D) To ask you to distribute pamphlets for the foundation.

The best answer to the question, "What is the speaker's purpose?" is *To inform you of the existence of the Health Research Center.* Therefore, you should choose answer (B).

Now listen to the next example.

<u>Sample Answer</u>

Why would you use the center's 800 number?

You will read: (A) To volunteer to distribute pamphlets.
(B) To make a contribution to the Health Research Center.
(C) To obtain a schedule of seminars.
(D) To ask questions regarding good health.

The best answer to the question, "Why would you use the center's 800 number?" is *To ask questions regarding good health.* Therefore, you should choose answer (D).

<u>Sample Answer</u>

GO ON TO THE NEXT PAGE

39. (A) The importance of fossil hunting.
    (B) Recent geological research in the States.
    (C) The geological connection between continents.
    (D) The finding of European fossils in America.

40. (A) In South Africa.
    (B) In South Carolina.
    (C) In South America.
    (D) In Southern Europe.

41. (A) Some European soil was left behind.
    (B) The Carolina slate belt appeared.
    (C) Some European fossils were found.
    (D) Some crab-like creatures appeared.

42. (A) They are still arguing.
    (B) They are very skeptical.
    (C) They are now convinced.
    (D) They are unconvinced.

43. (A) The discomforts passengers endured on the overland stage.
    (B) The improvements made by the Concord coach.
    (C) The historical use and importance of the overland stage.
    (D) The romance of the overland stage in Western legend.

44. (A) Blizzards.
    (B) Bandits.
    (C) Mechanical problems.
    (D) Fuel shortages.

45. (A) It is very important.
    (B) It is insignificant.
    (C) It will eventually be forgotten.
    (D) It is exaggerated.

46. (A) The prevention of heart disease.
    (B) Restricted diets for children.
    (C) Childhood feeding habits.
    (D) The age when heart disease strikes.

47. (A) To persuade the audience to contribute to the A.M.A.
    (B) To inform the audience about recent studies concerning heart disease.
    (C) To ask the audience to participate in the research on heart disease.
    (D) To control the audience's lifestyles and eating habits.

48. (A) Young children.
    (B) Middle-aged people.
    (C) Infants under two years old.
    (D) Children over two years old.

49. (A) Fat and salt.
    (B) Fat.
    (C) Salt.
    (D) Cholesterol.

50. (A) Too much salt in the diet.
    (B) An imprudent diet.
    (C) Fatty plaque in the arteries.
    (D) Low blood-cholesterol.

THIS IS THE END OF THE LISTENING COMPREHENSION SECTION OF THE TEST

THE NEXT PART OF THE TEST IS SECTION 2.
TURN TO THE DIRECTIONS FOR SECTION 2 IN YOUR TEST BOOK.
READ THEM AND BEGIN WORK.
DO NOT READ OR WORK ON ANY OTHER SECTION OF THE TEST.

SECTION 2
STRUCTURE AND WRITTEN EXPRESSION

Time – 25 minutes

This section is designed to measure your ability to recognize language that is appropriate for standard written English. There are two types of questions in this section, with special directions for each type.

<u>Directions:</u> Questions 1-15 are incomplete sentences. Beneath each sentence, you will see four words or phrases, marked (A), (B), (C), and (D). Choose the <u>one</u> word or phrase that best completes the sentence. Then, on your answer sheet, find the number of the question and fill in the space that corresponds to the letter of the answer you have chosen. Fill in the space so that the letter inside the oval cannot be seen.

Example I

    Sound comes in waves, and the
    higher the frequency, ...
    (A) higher is the pitch.
    (B) the pitch is higher.
    (C) the higher the pitch.
    (D) pitch is the higher.

The sentence should read, "Sound comes in waves, and the higher the frequency, the higher the pitch." Therefore, you should choose answer (C).

<u>Sample Answer</u>
Ⓐ Ⓑ ● Ⓓ

Example II

    Fire safety in family houses, ...
    most fire deaths occur, is difficult
    to achieve.
    (A) where
    (B) why
    (C) how
    (D) when

The sentence should read, "Fire safety in family houses, where most fire deaths occur, is difficult to achieve." Therefore, you should choose answer (A).

<u>Sample Answer</u>
● Ⓑ Ⓒ Ⓓ

After you read the directions, begin work on the questions.

GO ON TO THE NEXT PAGE ➡

1. Bees . . . . . display distinct preferences for different colors, but are also sensitive to ultra-violet light.
   (A) only
   (B) not only
   (C) only do
   (D) can only

2. . . . . . physicist, Gabriel Fahrenheit, invented the mercury thermometer in 1714.
   (A) There is
   (B) It is
   (C) The
   (D) It is the

3. Management . . . . . as the organization and coordination of an enterprise.
   (A) to be defined
   (B) it is defined
   (C) definable
   (D) can be defined

4. Jupiter . . . . . the largest planet in the Solar System.
   (A) is
   (B) which
   (C) although
   (D) being

5. When sugar . . . . . to yeast, fermentation takes place.
   (A) by adding
   (B) adding
   (C) it is added
   (D) is added

6. The overall efficiency of a system can be . . . . . that of its weakest element.
   (A) no greater than
   (B) less greater
   (C) nothing as great as
   (D) not the greater

7. The Puritans, ... percentage of the earliest settlers in Massachusetts, were a pious, self-disciplined people.
   (A) which size
   (B) a sizable
   (C) the sizable
   (D) that sizable

8. Deserts produce less than 0.5 grams of plant growth . . . . . from every square yard.
   (A) the day
   (B) some day
   (C) one day
   (D) a day

9. By observing REM, or rapid eye movements, ... to know when dreaming occurs during sleep.
   (A) it is the possibility
   (B) is the possibility
   (C) it is possible
   (D) then is possible

10. The Irish brought the popular custom of Halloween to America . . . . . 1840s.
    (A) into the
    (B) in the
    (C) within
    (D) during

11. At an experimental agricultural station, many types of grass are grown . . . . . various conditions.
    (A) under
    (B) underneath
    (C) below
    (D) beneath

GO ON TO THE NEXT PAGE ➤

12. Nitric acid . . . . . copper to give off brown fumes of nitrogen dioxide.
    (A) on reacting with
    (B) reacting to
    (C) reacts with
    (D) is reacting with

13. The saturated fat in dairy foods is thought . . . . . a factor in heart disease.
    (A) it is
    (B) to be
    (C) they are
    (D) as being

14. Robots are being used increasingly in industry as they can work on large jobs faster, are more precise and . . . . . .
    (A) don't as easily tire
    (B) don't tire more easily
    (C) don't tire easily
    (D) don't too easily tire

15. Many plants can grow in water, without any soil, ... nutrients are added.
    (A) as long as
    (B) sure that
    (C) above all
    (D) of necessity

<u>Directions:</u> Questions 16-40 each sentence had four underlined words or phrases. The four underlined parts of the sentence are marked (A), (B), (C), and (D). Identify the <u>one</u> underlined word or phrase that must be changed in order for the sentence to be correct. Then, on your answer sheet, find the number of the question and fill in the space that corresponds to the letter of the answer you have chosen.

Example I

After Newton <u>has observed</u> an apple <u>fall</u>
      A   B

to the ground, he formulated <u>the</u> law of
            C

<u>gravity</u>.
 D

The underlined words <u>has observed</u> would not be acceptable in carefully written English. The past perfect form of the verb should be used to express the first of two completed actions in the past. Therefore, the sentence should read, "After Newton had observed an apple fall to the ground, he formulated the law of gravity." To answer the question correctly, you should choose (A).

<u>Sample Answer</u>
● Ⓑ Ⓒ Ⓓ

GO ON TO THE NEXT PAGE ➡

Example II

In 1740, John Newbery was <u>the</u>
　　　　　　　　　　　　　　　A

first publisher <u>to produce</u>
　　　　　　　　　　B
books <u>which</u> children really
　　　　C
wanted <u>read</u>.
　　　　D

The underlined word <u>read</u> would not be accepted in carefully written English. The infinitive form to read should be used because the verb wanted takes an infinitive with "to." Therefore, the sentence should read, "In 1740, John Newbery was the first publisher to produce books which children really wanted to read." To answer the question correctly, you should choose (D).

<u>Sample Answer</u>
Ⓐ Ⓑ Ⓒ ●

After you read the directions, begin work on the questions.

16. Epsom salts, or epsonite, <u>belong</u> to the <u>same class crystals</u> <u>as</u> the <u>gem</u> topaz.
　　　　　　　　　　　　　　A　　　　　　B　　　　　　C　　　D

17. <u>Either</u> the storm or the spring tide <u>caused</u> flooding <u>in</u> <u>the</u> Carolina coast.
　　A　　　　　　　　　　　　　　　　B　　　　　　C　D

18. Although we are <u>no longer</u> young, we <u>still</u> <u>enjoy</u> <u>to study</u> languages.
　　　　　　　　　A　　　　　　　　B　　C　　　D

19. If you <u>have</u> an opportunity <u>to choose</u> your seat <u>in</u> the Listening Comprehension section of
　　　　　A　　　　　　　　　B　　　　　　　C
the TOEFL, <u>you choose</u> one near the speakers.
　　　　　　　D

20. Gemstone amber <u>is</u> the <u>fossil</u> sap <u>off</u> <u>ancient</u> trees.
　　　　　　　　　A　　　B　　　C　　D

21. <u>Before</u> the 1920s, scientists <u>use to</u> think an immobilized muscle <u>would</u> become <u>weaker</u>.
　　A　　　　　　　　　　B　　　　　　　　　　　　　C　　　　　D

22. <u>One</u> of <u>the first</u> rescue <u>methods</u> in space <u>were</u> called MOOSE – manned orbital operations
　　A　　　B　　　　　C　　　　　　D
safety equipment.

23. <u>The</u> ruins <u>of</u> Mayan cities have <u>recent</u> been discovered <u>in</u> the Mexican jungle.
　　A　　　B　　　　　　　　　C　　　　　　　D

GO ON TO THE NEXT PAGE

24. Breakdancing, <u>or say</u>, "some forms <u>of</u> dancing," <u>can</u> cause serious injuries, <u>according</u>
          A   B   C   D
chiropractors.

25. Nuclear waste has traditionally <u>been stored</u> in steel drums <u>what</u> <u>are</u> subject <u>to</u> rust.
                                A   B C   D

26. The immune system <u>is</u> the <u>bodies</u> way of protecting <u>itself</u> <u>against</u> viruses.
                   A   B   C   D

27. <u>One of</u> Hana Claus's <u>experiments</u>, a frothy ceramic <u>called</u> Beerstone, <u>was produced</u>.
   A   B   C   D

28. People <u>visiting</u> Los Angeles usually <u>take</u> a tour of Universal Studios, <u>go</u> to the Chinese
          A   B   C
Theater, and <u>looking</u> at the footprints of the stars.
        D

29. The videodisc <u>has</u> the capacity <u>to store</u> <u>thousand</u> <u>of</u> visual images.
             A   B   C   D

30. It <u>has been discovered</u> that when bananas are <u>completely</u> ripe or cooked, they are one of the
    A   B
most <u>digestion</u> foods, and of great value <u>in treating</u> certain diseases.
    C   D

31. During the Industrial Revolution, farmers <u>have left</u> <u>their</u> fields and <u>went</u> to work in <u>dimly-lit</u>
                                        A   B   C   D
factories and mines.

32. <u>Although discovered</u> the X-ray in 1895, Professor Roentgen <u>died</u> poor and <u>neglected</u> without
    A   B   C
any honors in his <u>lifetime</u>.
             D

33. In Northern America, <u>both</u> the bison and certain species of bear <u>is</u> on <u>their</u> way to <u>becoming</u>
                      A   B C   D
extinct.

34. <u>Originate</u> in Ethiopia, coffee <u>was drunk</u> in the Arab world before <u>it</u> <u>came</u> to Europe in the
    A   B   C D
17th century.

35. Amsterdam is a town <u>who</u> is sometimes <u>referred to</u> as the "Venice of <u>Northern</u> Europe"
                   A   B   C
because of <u>its</u> canals.
         D

GO ON TO THE NEXT PAGE ➤

36. A deep-orange <u>color</u> carrot, <u>rich in</u> vitamin A, <u>has been produced</u> at <u>the</u> University of
                    A   B   C   D
Wisconsin.

37. The sea wasp <u>releases</u> a poison <u>that</u> <u>kill</u> a person <u>in</u> three minutes.
                A   B C   D

38. <u>Many time</u> in geological history <u>the earth's</u> magnetic field has changed, <u>with</u> the north
    A   B   C
magnetic pole <u>becoming</u> the south, and vice versa.
                D

39. Pipe and cigar smoke is thought to be <u>at least</u> as dangerous as cigarette smoke; the
                                           A
<u>much important</u> and crucial determiner is <u>whether</u> you <u>inhale</u> the smoke.
      B   C   D

40. Halley's comet <u>approaches</u> the earth, <u>close</u> to be <u>visible</u>, <u>every</u> seventy-five years.
                  A   B   C   D

THIS IS THE END OF SECTION 2

IF YOU FINISH BEFORE TIME IS CALLED, CHECK YOUR WORK
ON SECTION 2 ONLY.
DO NOT READ OR WORK ON ANY OTHER SECTION OF THE
TEST.
THE SUPERVISOR WILL TELL YOU WHEN TO BEGIN WORK ON
SECTION 3.

3 · 3 · 3 · 3 · 3 · 3 · 3

SECTION 3
READING COMPREHENSION

Time – 55 minutes

This section is designed to measure your comprehension of standard written English.

<u>Directions:</u> In this section, you will read several passages. Each is followed by a number of questions about it. For questions 1-50, you are to choose the <u>one</u> best answer, (A), (B), (C), or (D), to each question. Then on your answer sheet, find the number of the question and fill in the space that corresponds to the letter of the answer you have chosen.

Answer all questions about the information in a passage on the basis of what is <u>stated</u> or <u>implied</u> in that passage.

Read the following passage:

The Mediterranean fruit fly is one of the world's most destructive insect pests. It attacks more than 250 kinds of fruits, nuts, and vegetables. If the pest made its way into fruit and vegetable-growing parts of the United States, supplies of produce would go down and prices would go up. It would devastate commercial agriculture and could cost consumers an estimated additional
5 $820 million per year.

Example I

What is the main idea of the passage?
(A) Farmers need to produce more as a result of the Medfly.
(B) Commercial agriculture is very expensive in the United States.
(C) People should be aware of the danger of the Medfly.
(D) Many fruits and vegetables are infested by the Medfly in the United States.

The main idea of the passage is to warn people about the danger of the Medfly. Therefore, you should choose answer (C).

Sample Answer
Ⓐ Ⓑ ● Ⓓ

Example II

In line 3, the word "It" refers to
(A) commercial agriculture.
(B) supplies of produce.
(C) The Mediterranean fruit fly.
(D) $820 million.

The word "It" refers to "if the pest made its way," the pest is the Medfly, so you should choose answer (C).

Sample Answer
Ⓐ Ⓑ ● Ⓓ

Now begin work on the questions.

GO ON TO THE NEXT PAGE ➤

Questions 1-10

The eyes of moles and some burrowing rodents are rudimentary in size, and, in some cases, quite
covered by skin and fur. This state of the eyes is probably due to gradual reduction from disuse,
aided perhaps by natural selection. In South America, a burrowing rodent, the tuco-tuco or
Ctenomys, is even more subterranean in its habits than the mole, and is frequently blind. One
5 which was kept alive was in this condition, the cause, as appeared on dissection, having been
inflammation of the nictitating membranes. As frequent inflammation of the eyes must be
injurious to any animal, and as eyes are certainly not necessary to animals having subterranean
habits, a reduction in their size, with the adhesion of the eyelids and growth of fur over them,
might in such a case be an advantage. Thus, natural selection would aid the effects of disuse.
10 It is well known that several animals, belonging to the many different classes, which inhabit the
caves of Kentucky, are blind. In some of the crabs, the foot-stalk for the eye remains, though the
eye is gone. As it is difficult to imagine that eyes, though useless, could be in any way injurious
to animals living in darkness, their loss may be attributed to disuse.

1. What does the passage mainly discuss?
   (A) The cause of blindness in some
       rodents of natural selection
   (B) The effect on some animals of
       living in darkness
   (C) The disuse of eyes causing disease
       in burrowing rodents
   (D) The lack of eyes being injurious to
       cave-dwelling crabs

2. It can be inferred from the passage that
   (A) physical changes in burrowing
       animals are mainly caused by their
       habitat.
   (B) an animal's mobility is dependent
       on its dwelling place.
   (C) evolution initiates physiological
       changes in rodents.
   (D) sight impaired animals have
       difficulty in operating normally.

3. The word "One" in line 4 refers to
   (A) eyes.
   (B) moles.
   (C) Ctenomys.
   (D) membranes.

4. According to the passage, some burrow-
   ing animals are born
   (A) without eyes.
   (B) completely blind.
   (C) with furry eyes.
   (D) without eyelids.

5. The word "subterranean" in line 4 is
   closest in meaning to
   (A) undercover.
   (B) secret.
   (C) elusive.
   (D) underground.

6. All of the following contribute to natural
   selection in burrowing animals EXCEPT
   (A) eye disease.
   (B) underground habit.
   (C) loss of eyes.
   (D) injurious lifestyle.

7. The word "adhesion" in line 8 is closest
   in meaning to
   (A) securing.
   (B) fastening.
   (C) binding.
   (D) sticking.

8. According to the passage, as rodents
   burrow deeper and deeper into the ground,
   they become
   (A) smaller.
   (B) sightless.
   (C) useless.
   (D) eyeless.

GO ON TO THE NEXT PAGE

9. It can be inferred from the passage that the foot-stalk of the crab probably
    (A) is the remaining part of the eye mechanism.
    (B is used by the crab to feel in the dark.
    (C) helps the crab move around in the cave.
    (D) is part of the crab's protective system.

10. Where in the passage does the author suggest that eyes of some animals have disappeared because they are no longer necessary?
    (A) Lines 3 - 4
    (B) Lines 4 - 6
    (C) Lines 7 - 9
    (D) Lines 12 - 13

Questions 11 - 20

The application of the science of genetics to plant breeding occupies a strategic place in the enhancement of crop productivity. Upon its success depends the effectiveness of many other efforts to provide adequate food supplies for direct consumption by man, feed for animals, and agricultural raw materials for industry. Bringing more water to the land, improving the soil,
5 providing plant nutrients, teaching better cultural practices, and providing more efficient tools, cannot yield maximum results unless the plants under cultivation are able to respond fully to the improved environment and practices.

    Plant breeders' main aims are the same throughout the world. Apart from evolving varieties with higher yield potentials, the usual main objectives are greater cultural reliability, greater
10 resistance to diseases and pests, adaptation to the special requirements of different types of cultural practices, and improvement of quality, both nutritional and industrial. Most of the scientific methods developed are equally applicable everywhere.

    Selections made from indigenous and imported materials will usually provide suitable seed populations for formal breeding work, which should be started on the broadest possible
15 heterogeneous, or diverse, base. Large collections of germ plasma of wheat, oats, barley, corn, rice, soya beans, lucerne, and other crops are normally available for breeding. Ultimate progress depends on developing populations which have the desirable combinations of genes and gene frequencies.

    To make sure of the presence of these genes, hybridization of carefully selected parents is necessary. Frequency of genes can be increased by various mating systems. Once the suitable
20 populations are available, success depends on effectiveness of selection. To ensure this, the differential effects of environment among the individuals must be reduced to a minimum.

11. What is the main topic of the passage?
    (A) Breeding selective genes in plants
    (B) Increasing productivity in crops
    (C) Improving the quality of the agricultural environment
    (D) Multiplying the number of genes in plants

12. The word "enhancement" in line 2 is closest in meaning to
    (A) extension.
    (B) advance.
    (C) increase.
    (D) development.

13. The expression "able to respond fully to" in line 6 is closest in meaning to
    (A) get the better of.
    (B) take advantage of.
    (C) make a profit from.
    (D) have a use for.

GO ON TO THE NEXT PAGE

14. Which of the following is NOT given as an example of a main aim of a plant breeder?
    (A) Breeding true
    (B) Cultural change
    (C) Healthier plants
    (D) Heavier cropping

15. The word "which" in line 14 refers to
    (A) scientific methods.
    (B) imported materials.
    (C) breeding work.
    (D) seed populations.

16. According to the passage it is important to
    (A) eliminate germs from the crops.
    (B) have a wide variety of plasma.
    (C) only use plasma from cereals.
    (D) develop crops from the same plasma base.

17. Why is hybridization so important?
    (A) It ensures suitable genes are combined.
    (B) It produces strong parent plants.
    (C) It makes it possible to split the populations.
    (D) It develops clones of parent plants.

18. The word "differential" in line 21 could best be replaced by
    (A) special.
    (B) subtle.
    (C) marginal.
    (D) diverse.

19. It can be inferred from the passage that success in breeding finally depends on
    (A) environment.
    (B) selection.
    (C) culture.
    (D) nutrition.

20. For which of the following terms does the author supply a definition?
    (A) "consumption" line 3
    (B) "indigenous" line 13
    (C) "broadest" line 14
    (D) "heterogeneous" line 15

Questions 21 - 30

The old view that every point of light in the sky represented a possible home for life is very foreign to modern astronomy. The stars have surface-temperatures of anything from 1,650 degrees to 60,000 degrees or more and are at far higher temperatures inside. A large part of the matter of
5 the universe consists of stellar matter at a temperature of millions of degrees. Its molecules are broken up into atoms, and the atoms broken up, partially or wholly, into their constituent parts. The rest consists, for the most part, of nebular gas or dust. Now the very concept of life implies duration in time. There can be no life – or at least no life similar to that we know on earth – where atoms change their makeup millions of times a second and no pair of atoms can every stay joined
10 together. It also implies a certain mobility in space, and these two implications restrict life to the small range of physical conditions in which the liquid state is possible. A survey of the universe has shown how small this range is in comparison with that exhibited by the universe as a whole. It is not to be found in the stars, nor in the nebulae out of which the starts are born. Indeed, probably only an infinitesimal fraction of the matter of the universe is in the liquid state.
15 Actually, we know of no type of astronomical body in which conditions can be favorable to life except planets like our own revolving around a sun. Even these may be too hot or too cold for life to obtain a footing. In the solar system, for instance, it is hard to imagine life existing on Mercury or Neptune since liquids boil on the former and freeze hard on the latter.

GO ON TO THE NEXT PAGE

21. What does the passage mainly discuss?
    (A) The possibility of life existing on certain planets
    (B) The necessity of a liquid state on planets
    (C) The improbability of life in the universe
    (D) The varied matter which exists in the universe

22. In the passage, stars are described as
    (A) possessing fluctuating temperatures.
    (B) being destroyed by atoms exploding.
    (C) having stable molecular matter.
    (D) consisting of nuclear gases and dust.

23. The phrase "for the most part" in line 7 can best be replaced by
    (A) at the maximum.
    (B) more than ever.
    (C) to a large extent.
    (D) more and more.

24. The word "It" in line 10 refers to
    (A) duration in time.
    (B) pair of atoms.
    (C) mobility of space.
    (D) concept of life.

25. It can be inferred from the passage that life in the universe
    (A) could exist in stellar matter.
    (B) requires special conditions.
    (C) can evolve from atomic mobility.
    (D) emerges from the nebulae.

26. The word "infinitesimal" in line 14 is closest in meaning to
    (A) compact.
    (B) minute.
    (C) uncountable.
    (D) partial.

27. All of the following were found in the survey of the universe EXCEPT
    (A) atoms are always found in pairs.
    (B) very little matter is in a liquid state.
    (C) life exists only in limited cases.
    (D) nebulae and stars are basically arid.

28. The word "these" in line 16 refers to
    (A) stars.
    (B) planets.
    (C) conditions.
    (D) liquids.

29. In line 17, which of the following could be referred to as "a footing?"
    (A) A toehold
    (B) A handgrip
    (C) Footmark
    (D) A headrest

30. Where in the passage does the author suggest that life in the universe was considered viable?
    (A) Lines 1 - 2
    (B) Lines 6 - 7
    (C) Lines 7 - 10
    (D) Lines 15 - 16

GO ON TO THE NEXT PAGE

Questions 31 - 40

In the body's blood system, the heart is the pump that does the vital job of circulating the blood to all parts of the body. The tubes or blood vessels which carry blood from the heart are known as arteries; the blood vessels that return the blood to the heart are veins. The heart is really two pumps side by side. Each pump sucks blood from veins into a collecting chamber, the atrium or
5 auricle, which then pushes the blood under high pressure into the ventricle below it. The ventricles pump the blood under high pressure into arteries. The pulse, which can be felt at various parts of the body, is caused by the simultaneous pumping action of the two ventricles.

Blood that has given up its oxygen to the tissues (deoxygenated blood) enters the heart through the right atrium. The right ventricle then pumps it to the lungs. Here it collects oxygen and returns
10 through the veins to the left side of the heart to be pumped to the rest of the body, before returning to the right atrium again. The double circulation is needed because the pressure has to be boosted by re-pumping through the heart, so that it can pass around the body fast enough to supply the body tissues with the necessary oxygen.

A very important role is played by small flaps of skin at the exits of the heart and between the
15 auricles and ventricles: these are one-way valves that prevent the blood going the wrong way. If these valves are faulty, it has a serious effect on the system, as blood seeps out from the flaps.

31. Which of the following is the main topic of the passage?
    (A) How the heart works
    (B) The blood system of the body
    (C) The importance of oxygen in the body
    (D) Why the heart has two pumps

32. The word "it" in line 8 refers to
    (A) blood.
    (B) pump.
    (C) atrium.
    (D) ventricle.

33. It can be inferred from the passage that the pulse is the
    (A) vibration of blood in the veins.
    (B) noise of the blood in the ventricles.
    (C) sound of blood vibrating in the ventricles.
    (D) rhythmical throbbing of the arteries.

34. The word "simultaneous" in line 7 is closest in meaning to
    (A) one at a time.
    (B) all the time.
    (C) at the same time.
    (D) all at once.

35. According to the passage, when the blood needs more oxygen it gets is from the
    (A) atrium.
    (B) veins.
    (C) tissues.
    (D) lungs.

36. The word "tissues" in line 8 could best be replaced by
    (A) living cells.
    (B) outer skin.
    (C) inner muscles.
    (D) weak blood.

37. Why is the blood passed through the right atrium twice?
    (A) To be reoxygenated
    (B) to increase the pressure
    (C) To boost the lungs
    (D) to speed up the heart's beat

GO ON TO THE NEXT PAGE ▶

38. The word "flaps" in line 14 is closest in meaning to
    (A) peel.
    (B) layers.
    (C) covering.
    (D) plugs.

39. According to the passage, if there is a fault in the valves, the blood
    (A) stops flowing.
    (B) changes course.
    (C) exits through the skin flaps.
    (D) goes into the lungs.

40. For which of the following terms does the author supply a definition?
    (A) Blood
    (B) Valves
    (C) Pulse
    (D) Lungs

Questions 41 - 50

Nowadays, mulitplex cinemas are a permanent and entrenched feature of shopping malls all over America and are becoming increasingly popular throughout the world. Many of the theaters are being expanded into entertainment complexes complete with virtual roller coasters, video arcades and food courts as well as a dizzying array of movie selections. At the Sony IMAX Theater in New
5 York City, the building's interior is a strange merging of high tech and nostalgia. As Mary Jane Dodge, the IMAX project director for Sony Theaters explains, "This is an homage to the great theaters of the past. With the Sony IMAX Theater, we want to take the past into the future." Walking into the complex, patrons are met by a 65-foot color mural collage of the great movie palaces. Downstairs, a smaller black-and-white mural depicts behind-the-scenes shots from famous films.
10 There is even a column used as a vertical time line which traces the major events in cinema history.
    Although the showcase of the complex is the IMAX Theater with its impressive 80-by-100-foot screen, personal sound devices, 3-D goggles, there are twelve additional theaters, ranging from 150 to 900 seats. They incorporate advanced technology into an architectural space designed "to create a cinema experience that has an entertainment value beyond the film," according to Robert Green,
15 a partner in the architectural firm that designed the complex. Each theater, designed around Hindu, Chinese, Moroccan, Olympic, Egyptian and other similar themes, is replete with ornate entrance portals and interior detailing, as well as state-of-the-art lighting and sound.

41. The word "virtual" in line 3 is closest in meaning to
    (A) powerful.
    (B) dangerous.
    (C) illusory.
    (D) high-flying.

42. With what topic is the second paragraph mainly concerned?
    (A) Advanced technology in the IMAX complex
    (B) What is incorporated in the IMAX complex
    (C) The design of the IMAX Theater

    (D) The architecture of the IMAX complex

43. From the passage it can be inferred that single movie theaters
    (A) provide good entertainment value.
    (B) mainly satisfy the general public.
    (C) have an old-fashioned design.
    (D) provide a high level of nostalgia.

GO ON TO THE NEXT PAGE

44. According to the passage, which of the following is NOT in the Sony IMAX Theater?
    (A) 65-foot color college
    (B) High tech equipment
    (C) Black and white mural
    (D) Colored film photographs

45. The word "This" in line 6 refers to
    (A) the IMAX Theater.
    (B) New York City.
    (C) the building's interior.
    (D) an homage.

46. What does Mary Jane Dodge mean when she says "we want to take the past into the future?"
    (A) Old films should be shown at the IMAX Theater.
    (B) The IMAX Theater pays respect to old films.
    (C) Old movie theaters should be modernized.
    (D) Old theaters should show modern films.

47. The word "depicts" in line 9 is closest in meaning to
    (A) illustrates.
    (B) explains.
    (C) describes.
    (D) outlines.

48. How is Robert Green's movie experience primarily different from a normal visit to a movie?
    (A) It offers a variety of movies to choose from.
    (B) It shows many aspects of the cinema and its history.
    (C) It demonstrates all the latest technology.
    (D) It gives the possibility of seeing unusual films.

49. The words "replete with" could best be replaced by
    (A) decorated with.
    (B) built with.
    (C) full of.
    (D) designed around.

50. By building cinemas around different themes, it can be inferred that the designers wanted to
    (A) indicate the universality of the cinema.
    (B) try out some new architectural ideas.
    (C) demonstrate which cinemas were showing foreign films.
    (D) add an extra dimension to movie going.

THIS IS THE END OF SECTION 3

IF YOU FINISH BEFORE TIME IS CALLED, CHECK YOUR WORK ON SECTION 3 ONLY.
DO NOT READ OR WORK ON ANY OTHER SECTION OF THE TEST.

TEST OF WRITTEN ENGLISH ESSAY QUESTION

Time – 30 minutes

Do you agree or disagree with the following statement?

WEALTH LEADS TO UNHAPPINESS.

Use reasons and specific examples to support your opinion.

PRACTICE TEST 2

SECTION 1
LISTENING COMPREHENSION

In this section of the test, you will have an opportunity to demonstrate your ability to understand conversations and talks in English. In this section, there are answers to all the questions based on the information heard.

Part A

<u>Directions:</u> In Part A, you will hear short conversations between two people. At the end of each conversation, you will hear a question about the conversation. The conversation and question will not be repeated. Therefore, you must listen carefully to understand what each speaker says. After you hear a question, read the four possible answers in your text book and choose the best answer to the question you heard. Then, on your answer sheet, find the number of the question and fill in the space that corresponds to the letter of the answer you have chosen.

Listen to an example on the recording:

Man:	**What seems to be the problem, ma'am?**
Woman:	**Well, the light switch is broken and a plug needs repairing.**
Question:	**What kind of work does the man probably do?**

In your book you will read: (A) He's a carpenter.
(B) He's a plumber.
(C) He's an electrician.
(D) He's an engineer.

From the conversation, you learn that the light switch is broken and a plug needs repairing. The best answer to the question, "What kind of work does the man probably do?" is *He's an electrician*. Therefore, the correct choice is (C).

<u>Sample Answer</u>
Ⓐ Ⓑ ● Ⓓ

1. (A) He didn't go to Chicago.
   (B) He had a good time in Chicago.
   (C) He spent his vacation here.
   (D) He didn't enjoy his trip.

2. (A) The weather is making her feel unwell.
   (B) She would like to go for a walk.
   (C) She doesn't feel well enough to go for a walk.
   (D) It's not very nice weather for a walk.

3. (A) If she can check her account.
   (B) If she can pay the bill by check.
   (C) If she can check the woman's accounting.
   (D) If she can have her purchases charged.

4. (A) He'll leave for class now and finish his paper later.
   (B) He'll finish his paper in class.
   (C) He'll go to class after he finishes his paper.
   (D) He wants to leave the class to begin his paper.

5. (A) He never drinks tea.
   (B) He prefers coffee at lunchtime.
   (C) He likes tea in the evening.
   (D) He doesn't drink coffee at lunchtime.

GO ON TO THE NEXT PAGE →

6. (A) At the check-in.
    (B) On the plane.
    (C) At the departure gate.
    (D) In front of the building.

7. (A) She thinks Cheryl is gaining weight because she doesn't exercise regularly.
    (B) She disagrees that Cheryl is gaining weight because she works at the gym.
    (C) She thinks Cheryl will lose weight now that she's started working at the gym.
    (D) She thinks Cheryl works out regularly with weights.

8. (A) Her sister works at the bakery.
    (B) The man is no judge of cakes.
    (C) She's surprised the man thinks she can cook.
    (D) Her sister bakes delicious cakes.

9. (A) She wants the man to repeat the question.
    (B) She is not very fond of Jack.
    (C) She doesn't understand the man.
    (D) She rarely thinks about Jack.

10. (A) Betty has a more difficult life than she does.
    (B) Betty would like to take care of her three boys.
    (C) Taking care of her three teenage sons is easy.
    (D) Betty's life is easy compared with her own.

11. (A) There's no problem.
    (B) He doesn't understand.
    (C) It's impossible.
    (D) He never lends money.

12. (A) In the credit department of a store.
    (B) At an airport check-in.
    (C) At the account inquiries counter at a bank.
    (D) At a supermarket checkout.

13. (A) He's the only one who doesn't have an assignment.
    (B) He thinks there is only one assignment for Friday.
    (C) Hc is in the same position as the woman.
    (D) He's the only one who can finish the assignment.

14. (A) All the dresses in that section have to be dry cleaned.
    (B) She shouldn't try to wash the polyester dresses.
    (C) She will have a problem finding a washable dress.
    (D) The polyester dresses in that section are all washable.

15. (A) Practice together.
    (B) Follow the director.
    (C) Locate the trouble.
    (D) Carry out instructions.

16. (A) Sales clerk.
    (B) Truck driver.
    (C) Computer operator.
    (D) Postal worker.

17. (A) Listen to the holiday traffic report.
    (B) Leave before the traffic gets too bad.
    (C) Try to be more like him.
    (D) Avoid leaving the building too early.

18. (A) Purchase the items for her.
    (B) Do her shopping for her.
    (C) Make a list of necessary items to shop for.
    (D) Relieve her of her items while she shops.

19. (A) Museum guide and visitor.
    (B) Bus driver and rider.
    (C) Librarian and library user.
    (D) Diplomat and government official.

GO ON TO THE NEXT PAGE

20. (A) During a play.
    (B) After a concert.
    (C) Before an exam.
    (D) After a lecture.

21. (A) What prompted the man to read the book.
    (B) Why the man was bored by the book.
    (C) How the man would describe the book.
    (D) Where the man was when he read the book.

22. (A) He's full because he's eaten enough salad.
    (B) He's lost weight and doesn't have to diet anymore.
    (C) He's tired of dieting and wants to stop.
    (D) He's eaten so much salad that he's going to have to diet.

23. (A) Mt. Washington has a very poor reputation.
    (B) Neither Mt. Washington nor Pike's Peak is well known.
    (C) Pike's Peak is the most famous mountain in the U.S.
    (D) The reputations of Mt. Washington and Pike's Peak are very different.

24. (A) She's amazed by what the man has told her.
    (B) She thinks the man has been given incorrect information.
    (C) She's accusing the man of lying.
    (D) She thinks the man can't get out of his predicament.

25. (A) Take the woman to the new gym.
    (B) Go see the new equipment at the gym.
    (C) Stop the woman from going to the gym.
    (D) Listen to the new workout tapes from the gym.

26. (A) The woman has given up her dream of being a teacher someday.
    (B) The woman didn't know how to teach, so she's going to write books instead.
    (C) The woman has never written books before.
    (D) The woman cannot do both teaching and writing.

27. (A) She thinks the man should talk to Professor Peterson about all the papers he's assigning.
    (B) She agrees that Professor Peterson is too hard on his students.
    (C) She thinks Professor Peterson doesn't know his subject matter.
    (D) She thinks Professor Peterson is helping them by assigning so many papers.

28. (A) Stockbroker.
    (B) Supermarket manager.
    (C) Sociology professor.
    (D) Jeweler.

29. (A) Write a check for the book she ordered.
    (B) Look to see if the woman's book order had arrived.
    (C) Put the woman's checkbook in order.
    (D) Write out an order for the woman's new checks.

30. (A) The true history of acupuncture.
    (B) What works are available on acupuncture.
    (C) Why acupuncture doesn't always work.
    (D) How acupuncture is used to cure disease.

GO ON TO THE NEXT PAGE

Part B

Directions: In this part, you will hear longer conversations. After each conversation, you will be asked several questions. You will hear the conversations and the questions about them only one time. They will not be repeated. Therefore, you must listen carefully to understand what each speaker says.

   After you hear a question, read the four possible answers in your test book and choose which one is the best answer to the question you heard. Then, on your answer sheet, find the number of the question and fill in the space that corresponds to the letter of the answer you have chosen.

   Remember, you should not take notes or write on your test paper.

31. (A) The location of the La Brea tar pits.
    (B) The discovery of ancient animal remains.
    (C) The exploration of the La Brea museum.
    (D) The description of prehistoric animals.

32. (A) The animals were drowned there.
    (B) The Spanish settlers threw them there.
    (C) The oil drillers left them there.
    (D) The animals were trapped there.

33. (A) In tar.
    (B) By the scientist.
    (C) In water.
    (D) By the depth of the pit.

34. (A) The Spanish settlers.
    (B) The oil drilling engineers.
    (C) The oil company scientist.
    (D) The archeologists in 1906.

35. (A) Go to the library and get books on prehistoric animals.
    (B) Go see the La Brea tar pits.
    (C) Try to find their own fossils.
    (D) Start roofing their house with tar from the pits.

36. (A) The merits of the Monterey Jazz Festival.
    (B) The history of jazz.
    (C) Louis Armstrong's contributions to jazz.
    (D) The difference between jazz and rock-and-roll.

37. (A) They're both taking the same bus.
    (B) They're both going to the Monterey Jazz Festival.
    (C) They both like rock-and-roll.
    (D) They both like Louis Armstrong.

38. (A) Composing jazz melodies.
    (B) Improvisation.
    (C) Artistry.
    (D) Playing the trumpet.

GO ON TO THE NEXT PAGE

Part C

<u>Directions</u>: In this part, you will hear various talks. After each talk, you will be asked several questions. The talks and questions will not be repeated. They will not be written out for you. Therefore, you must listen carefully to understand what the speaker says.

   After you hear a question, read the four possible answers in your test book and choose which one is the best answer to the question you heard. Then, on your answer sheet, find the number of the question and fill in the space that corresponds to the letter of the answer you have chosen.

Listen to this sample talk.

You will hear: **The National Health Research Center, perhaps more than any other organization, will directly affect the lives of millions of Americans every day. The Health Research Center volunteers will work all over the United States to provide information on diet and lifestyles. The bulk of the foundation's time will be spent conducting seminars and distributing pamphlets on how to prevent major illness and increase longevity. A free long-distance 800 number is available for anyone with health-related questions.**

Now listen to the following question.

What is the speaker's purpose?

You will read: (A)   To get you to join the foundation.
(B)   To inform you of the existence of the Health Research Center.
(C)   To persuade you to give a donation to the foundation.
(D)   To ask you to distribute pamphlets for the foundation.

The best answer to the question, "What is the speaker's purpose?" is *To inform you of the existence of the Health Research Center.* Therefore, you should choose answer (B).

<u>Sample Answer</u>
Ⓐ ● Ⓒ Ⓓ

Now listen to the next example.

Why would you use the center's 800 number?

You will read: (A)   To volunteer to distribute pamphlets.
(B)   To make a contribution to the Health Research Center.
(C)   To obtain a schedule of seminars.
(D)   To ask questions regarding good health.

The best answer to the question, "Why would you use the center's 800 number?" is *To ask questions regarding good health.* Therefore, you should choose answer (D).

<u>Sample Answer</u>
Ⓐ Ⓑ Ⓒ ●

39. (A) The personality of Hawthorne.
    (B) The subjects covered in Hawthorne's works.
    (C) Nathaniel Hawthorne's ancestry.
    (D) The life of Nathaniel Hawthorne.

40. (A) World History.
    (B) Psychology.
    (C) American Literature.
    (D) Theology.

41. (A) Socialism.
    (B) Prejudice.
    (C) Passion.
    (D) Guilt.

42. (A) Was determined to become a customs official.
    (B) Was dedicated to his writing.
    (C) Didn't like living in England.
    (D) Was not a religious man.

43. (A) Water vapor.
    (B) Skin odors.
    (C) Air currents.
    (D) Warmth and moisture.

44. (A) It quickly moves off in another direction.
    (B) It sends an electrical impulse to its central nervous system.
    (C) The pores in the hairs on its skin become blocked.
    (D) Its sensors become blocked by the water vapor in the repellent.

45. (A) A degree of instability in their use has emerged.
    (B) More research is needed into their efficiency.
    (C) They appear to be highly effective.
    (D) Their reliability has yet to be proved.

46. (A) To list the equipment necessary for the hike.
    (B) To describe the expected hiking conditions.
    (C) To talk about the view from the mountain summit.
    (D) To illustrate the dangers of climbing the mountain.

47. (A) Meteorologist.
    (B) Wilderness guide.
    (C) Landscape artist.
    (D) Travel agent.

48. (A) At the base of the mountain.
    (B) In a valley on the mountain.
    (C) At a rest stop on the mountain.
    (D) At the top of the mountain.

49. (A) They are usually mild.
    (B) Conditions are similar to those at the base of the mountain.
    (C) Conditions can be harsh.
    (D) They are constant and predictable.

50. (A) Thick forest.
    (B) Heavy brush.
    (C) Green meadows.
    (D) Low, sparse vegetation.

THIS IS THE END OF THE LISTENING COMPREHENSION SECTION OF THE TEST

THE NEXT PART OF THE TEST IS SECTION 2.
TURN TO THE DIRECTIONS FOR SECTION 2 IN YOUR TEST BOOK.
READ THEM AND BEGIN WORK.
DO NOT READ OR WORK ON ANY OTHER SECTION OF THE TEST.

SECTION 2
STRUCTURE AND WRITTEN EXPRESSION

Time – 25 minutes

This section is designed to measure your ability to recognize language that is appropriate for standard written English. There are two types of questions in this section, with special directions for each type.

Directions: Questions 1-15 are incomplete sentences. Beneath each sentence you will see four words or phrases, marked (A), (B), (C) and (D). Choose the one word or phrase that best completes the sentence. Then, on your answer sheet, find the number of the question and fill in the space that corresponds to the letter of the answer you have chosen. Fill in the space so that the letter inside the oval cannot be seen.

Example I

Sound comes in waves, and the
higher the frequency, ...
(A) higher is the pitch.
(B) the pitch is higher.
(C) the higher the pitch.
(D) pitch is the higher.

The sentence should read, "Sound comes in waves, and the higher the frequency, the higher the pitch." Therefore, you should choose answer (C).

Sample Answer
(A) (B) ● (D)

Example II

Fire safety in family houses, ...
most fire deaths occur, is difficult
to achieve.
(A) where
(B) why
(C) how
(D) when

The sentence should read, "Fire safety in family houses, where most fire deaths occur, is difficult to achieve." Therefore, you should choose answer (A).

Sample Answer
● (B) (C) (D)

After you read the directions, begin work on the questions.

GO ON TO THE NEXT PAGE

1. . . . . . is defined in terms of British Thermal Units or Btu for short.
    (A) The heat
    (B) Heat
    (C) It is heat
    (D) Although heat

2. Neither Alaska . . . . . border on any other state.
    (A) as well as Hawaii
    (B) or Hawaii
    (C) nor Hawaii
    (D) and Hawaii

3. Biologists tell us that the earth has seen 500 million species of animals . . . . . or so.
    (A) during the last 3 billion years
    (B) it was during the last 3 billion years
    (C) while in the last 3 billion years
    (D) since the last 3 billion years

4. . . . . . in California is Mt. Lassen, which has not erupted since 1914.
    (A) Only the active volcano
    (B) The active only volcano
    (C) The active volcano only
    (D) The only active volcano

5. The fuel savings . . . . . by adequate home insulation are very significant.
    (A) that accomplished
    (B) that can be accomplished
    (C) can be accomplished
    (D) can be so accomplished

6. The more distant a star happens to be, the dimmer . . . . . .
    (A) that seems to us.
    (B) seems to us.
    (C) seeming to us.
    (D) it seems to us.

7. . . . . . , Charles Goodyear, in 1829 discovered a method of vulcanizing rubber and by 1830 the rubber industry was firmly established.
    (A) A New England hardware merchant
    (B) He was a New England hardware merchant
    (C) Because a New England hardware merchant
    (D) A hardware merchant who was from New England

8. On September 9, 1850, California was admitted to the Union . . . . . .
    (A) being thirty-first state.
    (B) the thirty-first state.
    (C) for the thirty-first state.
    (D) as the thirty-first state.

9. . . . . . , plants use ordinary visible light to consume carbon dioxide from air and give off oxygen.
    (A) A process called photosynthesis which
    (B) Photosynthesis is a process by
    (C) By a process called photosynthesis
    (D) Photosynthesis is a process with

10. . . . . . the sense of smell can provide us with important signals, it is not nearly as useful as hearing.
    (A) Although
    (B) However
    (C) Still
    (D) Despite

11. The size of the pupil in the eye . . . . good indicator of a person's interest, emotion, attitude, and thought processes.
    (A) being the
    (B) is a
    (C) as the
    (D) the

GO ON TO THE NEXT PAGE ➤

12. Although Yosemite National Park is open all the year, ... come during the summer.
    (A) for the largest crowds
    (B) and the largest crowds
    (C) the largest crowds
    (D) but the largest crowds

13. *Child Care* is the most widely read child care manual ever written, and its author, Benjamin Spock, is the most famous pediatrician . . . . . .
    (A) ever living.
    (B) who lives.
    (C) ever lived.
    (D) who ever lived.

14. The American Indians wore little clothing from choice, ... for their fine soft deerskins and mantles of turkey feathers.
    (A) but were famed
    (B) and were famed
    (C) were famed
    (D) so were famed

15. The relative size of an insect's wing is much greater than . . . . . .
    (A) of a bird's wing.
    (B) that of a bird's wing.
    (C) a wing of a bird is.
    (D) that wing of a bird.

Directions: Questions 16-40 each sentence had four underlined words or phrases. The four underlined parts of the sentence are marked (A), (B), (C), and (D). Identify the one underlined word or phrase that must be changed in order for the sentence to be correct. Then, on your answer sheet, find the number of the question and fill in the space that corresponds to the letter of the answer you have chosen.

Example I

    After Newton <u>has observed</u> an apple <u>fall</u>
                         A   B
    to the ground, he formulated <u>the</u> law of
                                        C

    <u>gravity</u>.
     D

The underlined words <u>has observed</u> would not be acceptable in carefully written English. The past perfect form of the verb should be used to express the first of two completed actions in the past. Therefore, the sentence should read, "After Newton had observed an apple fall to the ground, he formulated the law of gravity." To answer the question correctly, you should choose (A).

<u>Sample Answer</u>
● Ⓑ Ⓒ Ⓓ

GO ON TO THE NEXT PAGE ➤

Example II

In 1740, John Newbery was <u>the</u>
                           A

first publisher <u>to produce</u>
                      B
books <u>which</u> children really
         C
wanted <u>read</u>.
          D

The underlined word <u>read</u> would not be accepted in carefully written English. The infinitive form to read should be used because the verb wanted takes an infinitive with "to." Therefore, the sentence should read, "In 1740, John Newbery was the first publisher to produce books which children really wanted to read." To answer the question correctly, you should choose (D).

<u>Sample Answer</u>
Ⓐ   Ⓑ   Ⓒ   ●

After you read the directions, begin work on the questions.

16. The <u>most</u> <u>bulkiest</u> of the poisonous snakes is the diamond <u>backed</u> rattler, which reaches 8 feet
        A   B   C
    8 inches <u>long</u>.
              D

17. <u>The</u> rice yields more food per acre than <u>any</u> other <u>grain,</u> and more people depend on <u>it</u> than any
    A   B   C   D
    other foodstuff.

18. The speed of light varies <u>considerably,</u> depending <u>on</u> the medium <u>through</u> which it is <u>moved</u>.
                              A   B   C   D

19. <u>The Comanches</u> were the most <u>skillful</u> horsemen of all the American Indians and ranked <u>as</u> the
    A   B   C
    most powerful <u>nomad</u> on the plains of the Southwest.
                  D

20. Trees <u>are</u> designed <u>as</u> <u>neither</u> hardwoods <u>or</u> softwoods.
          A   B   C   D

21. Copper was the first metal <u>used</u> by man and is still <u>of</u> strong demand <u>because</u> it is a good
                               A   B   C
    conductor <u>of</u> electricity.
              D

GO ON TO THE NEXT PAGE ▶

22. <u>In</u> 1872, Congress declared <u>that</u> Yellowstone <u>to be</u> the first <u>national</u> park.
    A   B   C   D

23. <u>Farming</u> now <u>use</u> 10 percent of the <u>earth's</u> land area to <u>produce</u> food.
     A   B   C   D

24. Ants and termites are <u>one other's</u> greatest <u>enemy</u>, ants always <u>being</u> the aggressors.
                         A B   C   D

25. In 1744, Benjamin Franklin <u>lead</u> in <u>the founding</u> of the American Philosophical Society, the
                                     A   B

    first <u>learned</u> society <u>of</u> America.
        C   D

26. Marian Anderson, one of the <u>world's</u> <u>finest</u> contraltos, had <u>some</u> of the great voices of
                                  A   B   C

    <u>all time</u>.
     D

27. <u>Among</u> bees, <u>the queen</u> is never alone, but is always surrounded by <u>a swarm</u> of workers, <u>whom</u>
    A   B   C   D

    guard, clean, and feed her.

28. Ozone is <u>extremely</u> active chemically and succeeds <u>in damaging</u> any vegetation <u>they</u> comes in
               A   B   C

    contact <u>with</u>.
         D

29. <u>The</u> right to vote <u>was granted</u> to women <u>after only</u> <u>the</u> adoption of the 19th Amendment
    A   B   C   D

    in 1920.

30. <u>Without</u> fungi, most green plants could <u>hardly</u> survive because <u>they</u> depend on the <u>produce</u> of
    A   B   C   D

    fungus decay in the soil.

31. The Social Security Act, <u>signed by</u> President Roosevelt in 1935, <u>was established</u> <u>old-age</u>
                             A   B   C

    benefits and unemployment <u>insurance</u>.
                            D

32. The novelist <u>who</u> <u>best</u> embodied the Jazz Age in <u>either</u> his personal life and <u>writings</u> was
               A B   C   D

    F. Scott Fitzgerald.

33. Magnesium <u>is</u> almost five <u>times</u> lighter than steel, so <u>it</u> is <u>wide</u> used in space vehicles and
               A   B   C D

    aircraft.

GO ON TO THE NEXT PAGE ➡

34. George Washington's <u>refused</u> to run <u>for</u> a third term established the custom that <u>no</u> President
                  A   B   C

    <u>should</u> serve for more than two terms.
    D

35. The natural conditions in the United States <u>which</u> most <u>affecting</u> manufacturers are
                                             A   B

    <u>factory power</u> and <u>labor</u> supply.
      C   D

36. In 1927, <u>the</u> revolution <u>struck</u> the motion picture industry <u>when</u> the first important <u>all-talking</u>
               A   B   C   D
    picture, *The Jazz Singer*, was a phenomenal success.

37. The <u>normal</u> credit card has a <u>magnetic</u> strip that holds 1,700 <u>bits</u> of <u>informations</u>.
        A   B   C   D

38. Powdered instant coffee was <u>on</u> the market, in some form <u>and</u> <u>another</u>, <u>long</u> before World War II.
                                 A   B C   D

39. In Yosemite National Park, <u>there is</u> a wall of granite called El Capitan which is <u>too</u> high <u>that</u>
                                  A   B   C
    it is almost three times <u>the height</u> of the Empire State Building in New York.
                              D

40. In the past, <u>some</u> of the most highly stressed <u>areas</u> in education <u>was</u> the moral <u>improvement</u> of
                  A   B   C   D
    students.

THIS IS THE END OF SECTION 2

IF YOU FINISH BEFORE TIME IS CALLED, CHECK YOUR WORK
ON SECTION 2 ONLY.
DO NOT READ OR WORK ON ANY OTHER SECTION OF THE
TEST.
THE SUPERVISOR WILL TELL YOU WHEN TO BEGIN WORK ON
SECTION 3.

SECTION 3
READING COMPREHENSION

Time – 55 minutes

This section is designed to measure your comprehension of standard written English.

<u>Directions:</u> In this section, you will read several passages. Each is followed by a number of questions about it. For questions 1-50, you are to choose the <u>one</u> best answer, (A), (B), (C), or (D), to each question. Then on your answer sheet, find the number of the question and fill in the space that corresponds to the letter of the answer you have chosen.

Answer all questions about the information in a passage on the basis of what is <u>stated</u> or <u>implied</u> in that passage.

Read the following passage:

The Mediterranean fruit fly is one of the world's most destructive insect pests. It attacks more than 250 kinds of fruits, nuts and vegetables. If the pest made its way into fruit and vegetable-growing parts of the United States, supplies of produce would go down and prices would go up. It would devastate commercial agriculture and could cost consumers an estimated additional
5 $820 million per year.

Example I

   What is the main idea of the passage?
   (A) Farmers need to produce more as a result of the Medfly
   (B) Commercial agriculture is very expensive in the United States
   (C) People should be aware of the danger of the Medfly
   (D) Many fruits and vegetables are infested by the Medfly in the United States

The main idea of the passage is to warn people about the danger of the Medfly. Therefore you should choose answer (C).

<u>Sample Answer</u>
Ⓐ Ⓑ ● Ⓓ

Example II

   In line 3, the word "It" refers to
   (A) commercial agriculture.
   (B) supplies of produce.
   (C) The Mediterranean fruit fly.
   (D) $820 million.

The word "It" refers to "if the pest made its way," the pest is the Medfly, so you should choose answer (C).

<u>Sample Answer</u>
Ⓐ Ⓑ ● Ⓓ

Now begin work on the questions.

GO ON TO THE NEXT PAGE

Questions 1-10

The bat, say scientists, is one of nature's most dazzling and precious creations. According to the fossil record, bats were soaring in the sky at least 55 million years ago. These ancient flyers, says evolutionary biologist Nancy Simmons of New York's American Museum of Natural History, were "virtually indistinguishable from today's echolocating bats." Though to look at them most
5 resemble rodents, bats' closest cousins are primates. Modern bats are amazingly diverse; about 1,000 species account for nearly a fourth of all mammal species. The only known group of flying mammals, they range in size from Thailand's tiny bumblebee bat, weighing almost nothing, to Indonesia's giant flying fox, with wingspans of nearly 5ft. Many bats feed on insects, while others prefer fruit, nectar, or pollen. A few feast on fish, frogs, rodents, and blood. Contrary to legend,
10 however, vampire bats, which dwell in Latin America, suck the blood of grazing cattle and horses, not sleeping humans.

Essentially docile, bats play a vital role in maintaining ecological balance. For one thing, they protect crops from marauding insects. The 20 million Mexican free-tailed bats that roost in Bracken Cave near San Antonio, Texas, from spring to fall consume 250 tons of insects every
15 night as they swarm to altitudes of more than 10,000ft. A single little brown bat can also lap up 600 mosquitoes an hour.

1. The passage primarily discusses the bat's
   (A) lifespan.
   (B) lifecycle.
   (C) lifestyle.
   (D) life-blood.

2. According to the passage, bats that lived 45 million years ago, compared with bats nowadays,
   (A) flew in a similar way.
   (B) flew higher in the sky.
   (C) had a different way of flying.
   (D) were unable to fly very high.

3. The phrase "virtually indistinguishable" in line 4 is closest in meaning to
   (A) absolutely identical.
   (B) closely resemble.
   (C) roughly equivalent.
   (D) approximately equal.

4. The word "they" in line 7 refers to
   (A) mammals.
   (B) bumblebees.
   (C) bats.
   (D) foxes.

5. The author mentions all of the following as food sources for bats EXCEPT
   (A) insects.
   (B) flowers.
   (C) reptiles.
   (D) birds.

6. The words "account for" in line 6 could best be replaced by
   (A) protect.
   (B) credit.
   (C) defend.
   (D) represent.

7. It can be inferred from the passage that vampire bats
   (A) exist only in legends.
   (B) behave unexpectedly.
   (C) prefer human blood.
   (D) have rarefied blood.

8. The word "marauding" in line 13 is closest in meaning to
   (A) contributory.
   (B) furious.
   (C) dangerous.
   (D) thieving.

GO ON TO THE NEXT PAGE

9. According to the passage, which of the following live in caves?
   (A) 20 million bats
   (B) 250 tons of insects
   (C) 600 mosquitoes
   (D) Small brown bats

10. Where in the passage does the author suggest there are old tales about bats?
   (A) Lines 1-2
   (B) Lines 2-5
   (C) Lines 9-11
   (D) Lines 13-16

Questions 11 - 20

Using the power of the sun to heat an enclosed space is an idea as old as humankind. Equally as old are the problems that go along with it. Cloudy weather makes for chilly conditions, while a surfeit of sunlight creates too much heat. An Albuquerque, New Mexico-based company, however, may have solved this age-old problem with a new device called a Weather Panel.

5 Suntek, founded in 1974 by Day Chahroudi, first burst upon the solar scene with Low-e, a transparent insulation for windows that prevented heat loss. Now Suntek has created a second material called Cloud Gel, a clear polymer that when heated to a certain temperature turns opaque and blocks sunlight. "A lot of atriums and sun spaces just become solar ovens," Day Chahroudi explains. "It's as if Cloud Gel makes sure the weather stays temperate, so a building cannot
10 overheat or be overbright."

The company's new Weather Panel, designed to be installed under a clear roof, consists of layers of Low-e and Cloud Gel, working in combination to let in "cloud light" – weak light that penetrates winter clouds – for heating and lighting and to reflect excess sunlight. The Weather Panel can be used on almost any building, and will cost no more than the average roof. It can also
15 provide one-sixth of the world's energy without pollution.

11. What does the passage mainly discuss?
   (A) Supplying part of the world's energy
   (B) The history of power from the sun
   (C) Methods of trapping the sun's energy
   (D) Ways of controlling the sun's power

12. The word "surfeit" in line 3 is closest in meaning to
   (A) capacity.
   (B) increase.
   (C) abundance.
   (D) excess.

13. The word "it" in line 2 refers to
   (A) humankind.
   (B) idea.
   (C) cloudy weather.
   (D) space.

14. According to the passage, which of the following is controlled by Cloud Gel?
   (A) Chilly conditions
   (B) Heat loss
   (C) Sunlight exclusion
   (D) Cloudy weather

15. What is meant by Day Chahroudi's statement in line 8?
   (A) It's possible to cook in atriums.
   (B) A space in the sun is ideal for cooking.
   (C) Hot sun can overheat atriums.
   (D) Too much heat can burn the buildings.

16. The word "opaque" in line 7 is closest in meaning to something which is
   (A) able to filter light.
   (B) impervious to light.
   (C) able to transmit light.
   (D) completely transparent.

17. According to the passage, the new Weather Panel is designed to
   (A) penetrate winter clouds.
   (B) work with clear roofs.
   (C) reflect cloud light.
   (D) admit sunlight.

GO ON TO THE NEXT PAGE

18. The word "it" in line 14 refers to
    (A) the world's energy.
    (B) any building.
    (C) the Weather Panel.
    (D) the average roof.

19. According to the author, a Weather Panel could be described as
    (A) a combination material device.
    (B) a clear polymer sheet.
    (C) a transparent installation.
    (D) a solar energy trap.

20. It can be inferred from the passage that the Weather Panel can do all of the following EXCEPT
    (A) contribute to the world's energy.
    (B) stop buildings overheating.
    (C) help prevent pollution.
    (D) protect roofs against cloudy weather.

Questions 21 - 30

Rocky Mountain Spotted Fever, an acute febrile illness, is transmitted to man by ticks. Prevention is attained primarily by avoidance of tick-infested areas. When this is impractical, personal prophylactic measures include the wearing of clothing which interferes with attachment of ticks, i.e., boots and a one-piece outer garment, preferably impregnated with a tick repellent, and daily
5 inspection of the entire body, including the hairy parts, to detect and remove attached ticks.
   In removing attached ticks, great care should be taken to avoid crushing the arthropod, with resultant contamination of the bite wound. Touching the tick with gasoline or whisky encourages detachment, but gentle traction with tweezers applied close to the mouth parts may be necessary. The skin area should be disinfected with soap and water or other antiseptics. Similarly, precautions
10 should be employed in removing engorged ticks from dogs and another animals, since infection through minor abrasions on the hands is possible. Vaccines are available commercially and should be used for those exposed to great risk, viz., persons frequenting highly endemic areas and laboratory workers exposed to the agent. Since the broad-spectrum antibiotics were shown to be such excellent therapeutic agents in Spotted Fever, there has been less impetus for vaccination of
15 persons who run only a minor risk of infection.

21. What is the main purpose of the passage?
    (A) To describe the symptoms of Spotted Fever
    (B) To explain how to treat Spotted Fever
    (C) To warn of the danger of Spotted Fever
    (D) To outline the types of Spotted Fever

22. The word "acute" in line 1 is closest in meaning to
    (A) fatal.
    (B) violent.
    (C) serious.
    (D) incurable.

23. From the passage, it can be inferred that ticks are
    (A) prickly plants.
    (B) biting animals.
    (C) poisonous reptiles.
    (D) blood-sucking insects.

24. The word "this" in line 2 refers to
    (A) prevention.
    (B) avoidance.
    (C) attachment.
    (D) clothing.

GO ON TO THE NEXT PAGE ➤

25. The author suggests all of the following as preventative measures against Spotted Fever EXCEPT
    (A) removing hair from the body.
    (B) dressing in suitable clothes.
    (C) staying away from infested areas.
    (D) using appropriate sprays.

26. The word "traction" in line 8 could be replaced by
    (A) dissection.
    (B) examination.
    (C) investigation.
    (D) removal.

27. The author states that most people become ill with Spotted Fever through
    (A) squeezing the body of a tick.
    (B) playing with dogs.
    (C) working in laboratories.
    (D) not washing with soap and water.

28. According to the passage, if whisky is applied to a tick, it
    (A) attaches itself to the mouth.
    (B) becomes very confused.
    (C) bites the person.
    (D) falls off the body.

29. The word "impetus" in line 14 is closest in meaning to
    (A) haste.
    (B) need.
    (C) chance.
    (D) thought.

30. The passage supports which of the following conclusions?
    (A) There is no known cure for Spotted Fever.
    (B) All people in the Rocky Mountains should be vaccinated.
    (C) Most medicines are ineffectual against Spotted Fever.
    (D) Spotted Fever is controllable with the use of suitable antibiotics.

GO ON TO THE NEXT PAGE

Questions 31 - 40

Farming has come a long way since the days of the horse-drawn plow, and now it's heading swiftly into the twenty-first century. Research at Indiana's Purdue University uses the Navstar Global Positioning System (GPS) to help increase crop yields and reduce chemical use. GPS uses satellite signals to determine locations within inches. Under Purdue's scheme, a farmer out in the
5 field would use a GPS receiver mounted on his vehicle to pinpoint his position. A computer linked to the receiver and programmed with the field's soil conditions – which can vary widely from one area to another – would tell the farmer precisely where the plant and how much pesticide and fertilizer to use at that specific site. "Currently, the number one cost to the farmer is chemicals," says Gary Kurtz, a Professor of Agricultural Engineering at Purdue. Site-specific
10 farming can increase yields while reducing chemical use.
    But the cost of this new technology may be too high for the small farmer. The cost of taking and testing soil samples every few feet in a farmer's field is a limiting factor. Soil tests can run $7 to $8 each. Mark Morgan, Assistant Professor of Agricultural Engineering at Purdue and his graduate assistants are working on a sensor to be attached to the front of a farm implement,
15 enabling the farmer to perform his own soil tests on the go.

31. What does the passage mainly discuss?
    (A) The rapid evolution of farming
    (B) Technological advances in agriculture
    (C) The problems of using computerized machines
    (D) The cost of new technology on farming

32. The word "it's" in line 1 refers to
    (A) a horse-drawn plow.
    (B) farming.
    (C) research.
    (D) Purdue University.

33. The word "yields" in line 3 is closest in meaning to
    (A) breeding.
    (B) formation.
    (C) performance.
    (D) conversion.

34. According to the passage, one of the main purposes of the GPS is to
    (A) help improve soil condition.
    (B) interpret satellite signals.
    (C) calculate costs of soil sampling.
    (D) select specific sites for planting.

35. It can be inferred from the passage that a farmer would use his computer to
    (A) contact Purdue University.
    (B) send messages to the satellite.
    (C) get specific information about sites.
    (D) interact with a sensor.

36. The word "pinpoint" in line 5 could best be replaced by
    (A) hold.
    (B) check.
    (C) locate.
    (D) steer.

37. Which of the following would be of NO value to increase crop yields?
    (A) Fixing a sensor to farm machinery
    (B) The use of a GPS receiver
    (C) Testing soil samples
    (D) The excessive use of chemicals

38. The expression "run to" in line 12 is closest in meaning to
    (A) pay back.
    (B) discount.
    (C) cost more.
    (D) amount to.

GO ON TO THE NEXT PAGE

39. According to the passage, the phrase "on the go" has the meaning of
    (A) sensing the time is right.
    (B) at the same time as planting.
    (C) preparing the soil.
    (D) while driving a plow.

40. What is the most expensive part of farming for farmers?
    (A) The cost of soil testing
    (B) The heavy use of chemicals
    (C) The use of technological systems
    (D) The purchase of modern equipment

Questions 41 - 50

Who was the man who first picked up a pebble and made it disappear? We owe that man a debt, for he was the first magician, the first to create wonder both intimate and real. He was the father of the oldest of all the performing arts.

5 Magic caters to a spirit of reverence and mystery, and it is the magician, above all other theatrical and performing artists, who must carry the torch of wonder. His art speaks to a primordial emotion inside us all. For magicians through the ages have instilled in wide-eyed children and even their jaded elders an almost lost-childhood sense of discovery.

Of all the performers on stage, no one courts disaster, no one flirts with failure as much as the magician. The juggler may drop a bowling pin, the singer may forget a lyric, the actor may fluff a

10 line, and all will be forgiven. But no magician is allowed to miss a trick without incuring derision from the audience.

An estimated 30,000 Americans have embraced magic as a hobby. There have been more books written on card magic alone than on any other performing art. Magic has invaded Broadway, television, the performing arts center, the rock concert, and the urban sidewalk. It is

15 the Golden Age of Conjuring.

Some of the finest minds to have ever existed have devoted their lives to creating new illusions. Gifted with intelligence, curiosity, and imagination, one can only wonder how the world might have changed had these conjurers chosen the fields of science or medicine in which to pour their genius.

41. What is the main purpose of the passage?
    (A) To consider magic as a celebration of mystery
    (B) To demonstrate some magical tricks which misfired
    (C) To discuss why many Americans practice magic as a hobby
    (D) To show that some magicians are also doctors or scientists

42. The word "create" in line 2 is closest in meaning to
    (A) involve.
    (B) direct.
    (C) produce.
    (D) suggest.

43. The words "above all" in line 4 refers to
    (A) magic.
    (B) spirit.
    (C) magician.
    (D) artists.

44. The author describes a magician as all the following EXCEPT
    (A) a conjurer.
    (B) an illusionist.
    (C) a genius.
    (D) a juggler.

GO ON TO THE NEXT PAGE ➤

45. According to the passage, all through the centuries, magicians have been able to
    (A) bewilder children.
    (B) confuse older people.
    (C) delight everybody.
    (D) invoke criticism.

46. The word "courts" in line 8 is closest in meaning to
    (A) avoids.
    (B) attracts.
    (C) regrets.
    (D) forgets.

47. It can be inferred from the passage that many Americans
    (A) enjoy playing cards.
    (B) hope to appear on television.
    (C) wish to act mysterious.
    (D) like to create illusions.

48. The word "invaded" in line 13 could best be replaced by
    (A) attacked.
    (B) overcome.
    (C) pervaded.
    (D) entertained.

49. In line 15, what does the author mean by the phrase "the Golden Age"?
    (A) An era of great prosperity
    (B) A period of great esteem
    (C) An age of much happiness
    (D) A time of perfection

50. The overall conclusion to be drawn from the passage is that the author thinks that magic is
    (A) a religious experience.
    (B) a theatrical act.
    (C) a mysterious force.
    (D) an eternal fascination.

THIS IS THE END OF SECTION 3

IF YOU FINISH BEFORE TIME IS CALLED, CHECK YOUR WORK
ON SECTION 3 ONLY.
DO NOT READ OR WORK ON ANY OTHER SECTION OF THE
TEST.

STOP STOP STOP STOP STOP STOP STOP

TEST OF WRITTEN ENGLISH ESSAY QUESTION

Time – 30 minutes

Do you agree or disagree with the following statement?

SOME STUDENTS LIKE TO SPEND THEIR VACATIONS WITH THEIR FAMILIES. OTHERS PREFER TO TRAVEL WITH THEIR FRIENDS.

Which type of vacation do you prefer?

PRACTICE TEST 3

1 • 1 • 1 • 1 • 1 • 1 • 1

SECTION 1
LISTENING COMPREHENSION

In this section of the test, you will have an opportunity to demonstrate your ability to understand conversations and talks in English. In this section, there are answers to all the questions based on the information heard.

Part A

Directions: In Part A, you will hear short conversations between two people. At the end of each conversation, you will hear a question about the conversation. The conversation and question will not be repeated. Therefore, you must listen carefully to understand what each speaker says. After you hear a question, read the four possible answers in your test book and choose the best answer to the question you heard. Then, on your answer sheet, find the number of the question and fill in the space that corresponds to the letter of the answer you have chosen.

Listen to an example on the recording:

Man: **What seems to be the problem, ma'am?**
Woman: **Well, the light switch is broken and a plug needs repairing.**
Question: **What kind of work does the man probably do?**

In your book you will read: (A) He's a carpenter.
(B) He's a plumber.
(C) He's an electrician.
(D) He's an engineer.

From the conversation, you learn that the light switch is broken and a plug needs repairing. The best answer to the question, "What kind of work does the man probably do?" is *He's an electrician*. Therefore, the correct choice is (C).

Sample Answer
(A) (B) ● (D)

1. (A) It is the only book for her philosophy class.
   (B) All the classes have a lot of reading.
   (C) She just has to read for her philosophy class.
   (D) Only the philosophy class has a lot of reading.

2. (A) He doesn't really have a degree.
   (B) He doesn't like to mention his engineering degree.
   (C) He must be smart if he has a degree.
   (D) He has a degree, but it took him a long time to get it.

3. (A) He agrees with the T.V. review.
   (B) T.V. reviews don't affect him.
   (C) He disagrees with the T.V. review.
   (D) T.V. reviews are always bad.

4. (A) At the school bookstore.
   (B) In the library.
   (C) In a classroom.
   (D) In the college office.

5. (A) He should get his hair blow dried.
   (B) He should get his hair cut a little.
   (C) He should get his hair tinted.
   (D) He should get a permanent.

GO ON TO THE NEXT PAGE

6. (A) New dances don't interest him.
    (B) He doesn't understand the rules of dancing.
    (C) He likes the new dances in particular.
    (D) All kinds of dancing are strange to him.

7. (A) Redo the copies.
    (B) Change the print setting.
    (C) Use a different machine.
    (D) Try out a darker paper.

8. (A) She'd like to turn on the T.V. early.
    (B) She wants to go to an early movie.
    (C) She doesn't mind the movies or T.V.
    (D) She wants to go to bed early.

9. (A) The single apartment is good value as it is cheaper.
    (B) He's prepared to pay more for the bigger apartment.
    (C) He is doubtful about the one-bedroom apartment although it is bigger.
    (D) There is a big difference between the two apartments.

10. (A) He doesn't feel like coffee.
    (B) He doesn't mind if she has coffee.
    (C) It doesn't bother him if she makes coffee.
    (D) He doesn't want the bother of making coffee.

11. (A) Send Mary a gift.
    (B) Present Mary with a gift.
    (C) Send a thank-you card to Mary.
    (D) Mail Mary a card of sympathy.

12. (A) She's a professional plumber.
    (B) She used to be a plumber.
    (C) She is used to fixing faucets.
    (D) She is too old to do plumbing.

13. (A) John calls her when he has a problem.
    (B) If he's away for three months, he calls her.
    (C) He calls her from New York when something is wrong.
    (D) He called her three months ago on his way to New York.

14. (A) If Phil's lucky, he might get a scholarship.
    (B) There is no way in which Phil can win a scholarship.
    (C) Phil's not going to chance his luck and try for a scholarship.
    (D) Phil's not being given a chance to get a scholarship.

15. (A) He's afraid the woman's car will damage his lawn.
    (B) He thinks the woman's car will crack his driveway.
    (C) He's worried in case he won't be able to get out in the morning.
    (D) He fears the woman will park badly as there is no light in the driveway.

16. (A) He had been working on his term paper in the library.
    (B) He went to another library to work on his paper.
    (C) The library wasn't open, so he couldn't work on his paper.
    (D) He had to finish his term paper, so he didn't go to the library.

17. (A) Why Marge would say such a thing.
    (B) Where Marge got her information.
    (C) When Marge made her remark.
    (D) Why Marge decided not to try out.

18. (A) Cooking a meal.
    (B) Conducting an experiment.
    (C) Fixing a car.
    (D) Cleaning a room.

19. (A) Learn how to sail.
    (B) Stay home.
    (C) Get sick.
    (D) Join his friends.

GO ON TO THE NEXT PAGE

20. (A) He's a biologist.
    (B) He's a dentist.
    (C) He's an historian.
    (D) He's an astronomer.

21. (A) Her class schedule is much easier than last semester's.
    (B) She's so busy she doesn't have time for a piece of cake.
    (C) Working so hard is making her hungry.
    (D) She wishes her classes were as easy as they used to be.

22. (A) Go buy popcorn.
    (B) Stay in the ticket line.
    (C) Leave the theater.
    (D) Congratulate the woman for her great idea.

23. (A) She won't repeat her mistake.
    (B) She's learned how to keep her leg in a cast.
    (C) She realizes she needs lessons.
    (D) She wishes she had taken lessons.

24. (A) Go outside and talk to him.
    (B) Look at his jacket to see if he needs a new one.
    (C) Check the weather to see if it's cold.
    (D) Go get his jacket that he left outside.

25. (A) She thinks the man needs to exercise.
    (B) She is knowledgeable about equipment and fitness.
    (C) She wishes she had an exercise machine.
    (D) She knows more than the man knows about the exercise machine.

26. (A) Rosey will find someone to write her paper at the planetarium.
    (B) Rosey should help the planetarium with their exhibits on meteors.
    (C) Rosey should leave immediately for the planetarium before the exhibit is gone.
    (D) Rosey might get some information for her paper at the planetarium.

27. (A) The man needs to remember to take his final.
    (B) The man might get a B on his final.
    (C) The man's grade could change after he takes his final.
    (D) The man isn't going to get out of taking his final, even though he has a B average.

28. (A) Learning to ride a horse.
    (B) Playing in a band for the first time.
    (C) Taking karate lessons.
    (D) Being taught how to drive a truck.

29. (A) Stick with his schedule.
    (B) Have lunch with his friends.
    (C) Go to the music class.
    (D) Take time to make out his schedule.

30. (A) She'd rather help the instructors than take the classes.
    (B) She'll take summer courses only if she needs extra help.
    (C) She can't help but take summer courses.
    (D) She'd rather not take any summer courses.

GO ON TO THE NEXT PAGE

Part B

Directions: In this part, you will hear longer conversations. After each conversation, you will be asked several questions. You will hear the conversations and the questions about them only one time. They will not be repeated. Therefore, you must listen carefully to understand what each speaker says.

After you hear a question, read the four possible answers in your test book and choose which one is the best answer to the question you heard. Then, on your answer sheet, find the number of the question and fill in the space that corresponds to the letter of the answer you have chosen.

Remember, you should not take notes or write on your test paper.

31. (A) Riders who went from coast to coast.
    (B) The name of a legend of the West.
    (C) A mail delivery service.
    (D) The story in a movie.

32. (A) One man died and that time it didn't.
    (B) On about 80 occasions it didn't.
    (C) There were just a few times it didn't.
    (D) It always reached its destination.

33. (A) When telegraph communication started.
    (B) Eighteen months after telegraph communication started.
    (C) Seven days after telegraph communication started.
    (D) After it had been in operation for only a week.

34. (A) The quality of Jack's new earphones.
    (B) The uses of scientific instruments under the sea.
    (C) The sounds made by sea-dwelling animals.
    (D) The anatomy of whales, dolphins, and crabs.

35. (A) Interested.
    (B) Bored.
    (C) Frightened.
    (D) Repulsed.

36. (A) They make louder noises than land-dwelling animals.
    (B) They have special muscles for swimming.
    (C) They communicate through sound.
    (D) The sounds they make are like rock music.

37. (A) Lasers.
    (B) Hydrophones.
    (C) Periscopes.
    (D) Underwater cameras.

38. (A) Drumming.
    (B) Whistling and clicking.
    (C) Long, loud song.
    (D) Rubbing and clapping.

GO ON TO THE NEXT PAGE

Part C

<u>Directions</u>: In this part, you will hear various talks. After each talk, you will be asked several questions. The talks and questions will not be repeated. They will not be written out for you. Therefore, you must listen carefully to understand what the speaker says.

After you hear a question, read the four possible answers in your test book and choose which one is the best answer to the question you heard. Then, on your answer sheet, find the number of the question and fill in the space that corresponds to the letter of the answer you have chosen.

Listen to this sample talk.

You will hear: **The National Health Research Center, perhaps more than any other organization, will directly affect the lives of millions of Americans every day. The Health Research Center volunteers will work all over the United States to provide information on diet and lifestyles. The bulk of the foundation's time will be spent conducting seminars and distributing pamphlets on how to prevent major illness and increase longevity. A free long-distance 800 number is available for anyone with health-related questions.**

Now listen to the following question.

What is the speaker's purpose?

You will read: (A) To get you to join the foundation.
(B) To inform you of the existence of the Health Research Center.
(C) To persuade you to give a donation to the foundation.
(D) To ask you to distribute pamphlets for the foundation.

The best answer to the question, "What is the speaker's purpose?" is *To inform you of the existence of the Health Research Center.* Therefore, you should choose answer (B).

Sample Answer
Ⓐ ● Ⓒ Ⓓ

Now listen to the next example.

Why would you use the center's 800 number?

You will read: (A) To volunteer to distribute pamphlets.
(B) To make a contribution to the Health Research Center.
(C) To obtain a schedule of seminars.
(D) To ask questions regarding good health.

The best answer to the question, "Why would you use the center's 800 number?" is *To ask questions regarding good health.* Therefore, you should choose answer (D).

Sample Answer
Ⓐ Ⓑ Ⓒ ●

GO ON TO THE NEXT PAGE

39. (A) How crocodiles reproduce.
    (B) The similarities between crocodiles and dinosaurs.
    (C) The characteristics of crocodiles.
    (D) The hunting habits of crocodiles.

40. (A) In a laboratory.
    (B) At a museum.
    (C) In a lecture hall.
    (D) At a zoo.

41. (A) Skull structure.
    (B) Teeth.
    (C) Large hind legs.
    (D) A water habitat.

42. (A) Animal behavior.
    (B) Imprinting.
    (C) Birds' habits.
    (D) Salmon spawning.

43. (A) Sociology.
    (B) Health.
    (C) Biology.
    (D) Geology.

44. (A) The object has the right color.
    (B) The object has a certain shape.
    (C) The object has motion.
    (D) The object contrasts with its surroundings.

45. (A) They are compelled to follow their mother figure.
    (B) It helps them find their home stream to spawn.
    (C) It impels them to hatch in the ocean.
    (D) Newly hatched fish are able to find their way to the sea.

46. (A) At a college bookstore.
    (B) In a college library.
    (C) In the students' common room.
    (D) In the staff common room.

47. (A) Disapproving.
    (B) Enthusiastic.
    (C) Persuasive.
    (D) Objective.

48. (A) Request a search be made.
    (B) Check the card catalog.
    (C) Ask for help at the circulation counter.
    (D) Go to the reference desk.

49. (A) Place a hold on it.
    (B) Ask for it to be recalled.
    (C) Ask for it to be mailed to you.
    (D) Request a search.

50. (A) They are there only to check out books.
    (B) Their job includes providing assistance.
    (C) Their main responsibility is to keep the shelves stacked.
    (D) Most of them work at the Reference Desk.

THIS IS THE END OF THE LISTENING COMPREHENSION SECTION OF THE TEST

THE NEXT PART OF THE TEST IS SECTION 2.
TURN TO THE DIRECTIONS FOR SECTION 2 IN YOUR TEST BOOK.
READ THEM AND BEGIN WORK.
DO NOT READ OR WORK ON ANY OTHER SECTION OF THE TEST.

2 • 2 • 2 • 2 • 2 • 2 • 2

SECTION 2
STRUCTURE AND WRITTEN EXPRESSION

Time – 25 minutes

This section is designed to measure your ability to recognize language that is appropriate for standard written English. There are two types of questions in this section, with special directions for each type.

Directions: Questions 1-15 are incomplete sentences. Beneath each sentence you will see four words or phrases, marked (A), (B), (C), and (D). Choose the one word or phrase that best completes the sentence. Then, on your answer sheet, find the number of the question and fill in the space that corresponds to the letter of the answer you have chosen. Fill in the space so that the letter inside the oval cannot be seen.

Example I

    Sound comes in waves, and the
    higher the frequency, ...
    (A) higher is the pitch.
    (B) the pitch is higher.
    (C) the higher the pitch.
    (D) pitch is the higher.

The sentence should read, "Sound comes in waves, and the higher the frequency, the higher the pitch." Therefore, you should choose answer (C).

Sample Answer

    Ⓐ Ⓑ ● Ⓓ

Example II

    Fire safety in family houses, ...
    most fire deaths occur, is difficult
    to achieve.
    (A) where
    (B) why
    (C) how
    (D) when

The sentence should read, "Fire safety in family houses, where most fire deaths occur, is difficult to achieve." Therefore, you should choose answer (A).

Sample Answer

    ● Ⓑ Ⓒ Ⓓ

After you read the directions, begin work on the questions.

GO ON TO THE NEXT PAGE ➤

1. . . . . . glaciers of the world occupy about 10 percent of the total land area.
   (A) As the
   (B) The
   (C) It is the
   (D) There are

2. Many animals use odors for identification, ... , sexual attraction, alarm, and a variety of other purposes.
   (A) the territorial marking
   (B) they mark territory
   (C) territorial marking
   (D) mark territory

3. Yosemite Valley, ... , was carved out by a glacier in the Ice Age.
   (A) there is now a National Park
   (B) it is now a National Park
   (C) is now a National Park
   (D) which is now a National Park

4. Ozone . . . . . extremely active chemically, and succeeds in damaging any vegetation it comes in contact with.
   (A) is
   (B) being
   (C) which is
   (D) by being

5. . . . . . tornadoes occur in many regions of the world, they are most prevalent in the United States.
   (A) As
   (B) Although
   (C) Yet
   (D) Since

6. Cellulose, ... , is one of the many substances known as carbohydrates.
   (A) is the building block of plant cell walls
   (B) it's the building block of plant cell walls
   (C) the building block of plant cell walls
   (D) by the building block of plant cell walls

7. The name Oklahoma is synonymous with the word "Indian" as it comes from Okla-homma . . . . . "red people."
   (A) meaning
   (B) by meaning
   (C) means
   (D) to mean

8. . . . . . , Elias Howe of Massachusetts constructed a sewing machine, upon which improvements shortly were made by Isaac Singer.
   (A) It was in 1846
   (B) In 1846 he was
   (C) In 1846
   (D) In 1846 was

9. Temperature inversions often occur when . . . . . in the late afternoon.
   (A) the earth's surface is cooled
   (B) earth's surface is cooled
   (C) also the earth's surface is cooled
   (D) that the earth's surface is cooled

10. Over 1,900 years ago, ... , who worked in Alexandria, Egypt, classified the stars by their brightness.
    (A) he is a Greek astronomer named Ptolemy
    (B) it was a Greek astronomer named Ptolemy
    (C) a Greek astronomer named Ptolemy
    (D) a Greek astronomer whose name was Ptolemy

11. . . . . . gold, silver, copper, and platinum, nuggets of pure iron are rarely found in nature.
    (A) As unlike
    (B) Unlike the
    (C) Unlike
    (D) Unlikely

GO ON TO THE NEXT PAGE ▶

12. By 1830, iron plows were in such great demand . . . . . , two factories in Pittsburgh alone turning out nearly 35,000 a year.
   (A) that was mass production
   (B) that they were mass produced
   (C) that were mass produced
   (D) it was mass production

13. Benjamin Franklin was not only a scientist, philosopher, and inventor . . . . . a craftsman, humanitarian, and essayist.
   (A) as well
   (B) also
   (C) and also
   (D) but also

14. Transfer of information takes place . . . . . in some way to the material that was originally learned.
   (A) only if the new material is similar
   (B) when is the new material similar
   (C) only with similar new material
   (D) so the similar new material

15. Fog was caused by the cooling of air until its water vapor condenses . . . . . microscopic waste droplets or ice-crystals.
   (A) forms
   (B) to be formed
   (C) to form
   (D) forming

Directions: Questions 16-40 each sentence had four underlined words or phrases. The four underlined parts of the sentence are marked (A), (B), (C), and (D). Identify the one underlined word or phrase that must be changed in order for the sentence to be correct. Then, on your answer sheet, find the number of the question and fill in the space that corresponds to the letter of the answer you have chosen.

Example I

   After Newton <u>has observed</u> an apple <u>fall</u>
                        A   B
   to the ground, he formulated <u>the</u> law of
                                  C

   <u>gravity</u>.
     D

The underlined words <u>has observed</u> would not be acceptable in carefully written English; the past perfect form of the verb should be used to express the first of two completed actions in the past. Therefore, the sentence should read, "After Newton had observed an apple fall to the ground, he formulated the law of gravity." To answer the question correctly, you should choose (A).

<u>Sample Answer</u>
● Ⓑ Ⓒ Ⓓ

GO ON TO THE NEXT PAGE

Example II

In 1740, John Newbery was <u>the</u>
                           A

first publisher to produce
                     B

books <u>which</u> children really
          C

wanted <u>read</u>.
        D

The underlined word <u>read</u> would not be accepted in carefully written English. The infinitive form to read should be used because the verb wanted takes an infinitive with "to." Therefore, the sentence should read, "In 1740, John Newbery was the first publisher to produce books which children really wanted to read." To answer the question correctly, you should choose (D).

<u>Sample Answer</u>
Ⓐ Ⓑ Ⓒ ●

After you read the directions, begin work on the questions.

16. <u>Except for</u> turkey at Thanksgiving, <u>no</u> single dish has gained wide enough popularity in the
     A   B
U.S. <u>to become</u> a <u>symbolic</u> for the country as a whole.
      C   D

17. Charcoal is <u>odorless</u> and <u>tastelessness,</u> and has <u>the</u> ability to absorb a <u>large</u> quantity of gas.
               A   B   C   D

18. Ginger <u>is</u> <u>three time</u> as hot as cumin, but <u>not as</u> hot as <u>chili powder</u>.
         A   B   C   D

19. <u>The</u> Fair Labor Standards Act, signed by President Roosevelt in 1938, <u>providing</u> <u>for</u> a
     A   B   C
minimum wage and a <u>40-hour</u> work week.
                     D

20. The <u>sense of</u> equilibrium depends <u>of</u> <u>sense</u> organs <u>in</u> the inner ear called semi-circular canals.
         A   B C   D

21. Ants find <u>their</u> way by following <u>scent</u> laid down by <u>their</u> previous <u>ants</u>.
            A   B   C   D

22. The <u>larger</u> region in <u>the U.S.</u> <u>for</u> wine-growing <u>is situated</u> in California.
        A   B C   D

23. Children will walk <u>at</u> about the same age whether <u>or</u> <u>no</u> they are <u>"taught"</u> by their parents.
               A   B C   D

GO ON TO THE NEXT PAGE ▶

24. In process of photosynthesis, all green plants absorb carbon dioxide gas in the manufacture
     A   B   C
    of food.
        D

25. Thomas Edison made improvements in the Crookes tube and became known for the inventor
                    A   B   C
    of the fluoroscope.
     D

26. Jazz includes not only Dixieland, the original name for this music, also bebop, progressive
         A   B   C   D
    jazz, swing, and boogie-woogie.

27. The first vaccine ever developed used to combat smallpox, a disease resulting from infection
                    A   B   C
    by a virus.
     D

28. The postwar decade marked by the advent of television, as the twenties were by that of radio.
                     A   B   C   D

29. Cocoa pods grow on the trunk and branch of the tree.
     A   B   C   D

30. The rust of iron and steel is essentially a chemical process.
     A   B C   D

31. Sponges attach themselves to the sea-floor and use internal moving parts to circulate water
     A   B   C
    and food towards them.
              D

32. In the 1840s, Joseph Henry, the most original American scientist since Benjamin Franklin,
     A   B   C
    made important discovery in electromagnetism.
               D

33. Before 1900, golf and tennis were almost complete participant rather than spectator sports.
                                 A   B   C   D

34. One of the most widespread uses of survey research today is for them rating radio, and
     A   B   C   D
    television programs.

35. The principle of radiocarbon dating is the most important science technique to be applied to
                              A   B   C
    archeological work in recent times.
                       D

GO ON TO THE NEXT PAGE ➤

36. <u>Making</u> cloth from synthetic fibers <u>is requiring</u> less labor than <u>making</u> <u>cloth</u> from natural fibers.
    A   B   C   D

37. Although oil and water can be mixed <u>temporarily</u> by <u>sufficiently</u> agitation, the mixture separates
                                            A   B

<u>rapidly</u> if <u>allowed</u> to stand.
  C   D

38. Death Valley, in California, <u>which</u> <u>it is</u> 280 feet below sea level, <u>is</u> the lowest spot <u>in the</u>
                                A   B   C   D

United States.

39. Uncle Sam is a nickname which <u>was used</u> <u>during first</u> the War of 1812 <u>to represent</u> the U.S.
                                   A   B   C

Government <u>and the</u> American people.
        D

40. Charles A. Lindbergh made the first <u>one-man,</u> <u>non-stopped</u> <u>flight</u> <u>across</u> the Atlantic Ocean
                                      A   B   C   D

in 1927.

THIS IS THE END OF SECTION 2

IF YOU FINISH BEFORE TIME IS CALLED, CHECK YOUR WORK
ON SECTION 2 ONLY.
DO NOT READ OR WORK ON ANY OTHER SECTION OF THE
TEST.
THE SUPERVISOR WILL TELL YOU WHEN TO BEGIN WORK ON
SECTION 3.

3 • 3 • 3 • 3 • 3 • 3 • 3

SECTION 3
READING COMPREHENSION

Time – 55 minutes

This section is designed to measure your comprehension of standard written English.

<u>Directions:</u> In this section, you will read several passages. Each is followed by a number of questions about it. For questions 1-50, you are to choose the <u>one</u> best answer, (A), (B), (C), or (D), to each question. Then on your answer sheet, find the number of the question and fill in the space that corresponds to the letter of the answer you have chosen.

Answer all questions about the information in a passage on the basis of what is <u>stated</u> or <u>implied</u> in that passage.

Read the following passage:

The Mediterranean fruit fly is one of the world's most destructive insect pests. It attacks more than 250 kinds of fruits, nuts, and vegetables. If the pest made its way into fruit and vegetable-growing parts of the United States, supplies of produce would go down and prices would go up. It would devastate commercial agriculture and could cost consumers an estimated additional $820 million per year.

5

Example I

What is the main idea of the passage?
(A) Farmers need to produce more as a result of the Medfly.
(B) Commercial agriculture is very expensive in the United States.
(C) People should be aware of the danger of the Medfly.
(D) Many fruits and vegetables are infested by the Medfly in the United States.

The main idea of the passage is to warn people about the danger of the Medfly. Therefore, you should choose answer (C).

<u>Sample Answer</u>
Ⓐ Ⓑ ● Ⓓ

Example II

In line 3, the word "It" refers to
(A) commercial agriculture.
(B) supplies of produce.
(C) The Mediterranean fruit fly.
(D) $820 million.

The word "It" refers to "if the pest made its way," the pest is the Medfly, so you should choose answer (C).

<u>Sample Answer</u>
Ⓐ Ⓑ ● Ⓓ

Now begin work on the questions.

Questions 1 -10

There are desert plants which survive the dry season in the form of inactive seeds. There are also desert insects which survive as inactive larvae or pupae. In addition, difficult as it is to believe, there are desert fish which can survive through years of drought in the form of inactive eggs. These are shrimps that live in the Mojave Desert, an intensely dry region in the southwest of the
5 United States where shade temperatures of over 50°C are often recorded.

The eggs are the size and have the appearance of grains of sand. When sufficient spring rain falls to form a lake, once every two to five years, these eggs hatch. Then the water soon swarms with millions of tiny shrimps about a millimeter long which feed on microscopic plant and animal organisms which grow in the temporary desert lake. Within a week, the shrimps grow from their
10 original 1 millimeter to a length of about 1½ centimeters.

Throughout the time that the shrimps are rapidly maturing, the water in the lake equally rapidly evaporates. Therefore, it is a race against time. By the twelfth day, when they are about 3 centimeters long, hundreds of tiny eggs form on the underbodies of the females. Usually, by this time, all that remains of the lake is a large, muddy patch of wet soil. On the thirteenth day and the
15 next, during the final hours of their brief lives, the females lay their eggs in the mud. Then, having ensured that their species will survive, the shrimps die as the last of the water evaporates.

If sufficient rain falls the following year to form another lake, the eggs hatch, and once again the cycle of growth, adulthood, egg-laying, and death is rapidly passed through. If there is insufficient rain to form a lake, the eggs lie dormant for a year, or even longer if necessary.
20 Occasionally, perhaps twice in a hundred years, sufficient rain falls to form a deep lake that lasts a month or more. In this case, the species passes through two cycles of growth, egg-laying and death. Thus the species multiplies considerably, which further ensures its survival.

1. What does the passage mainly discuss?
    (A) The effects of drought in the desert
    (B) The lifespan of fish eggs in desert conditions
    (C) The survival of insects in a desert climate
    (D) The importance of deep lakes in the desert

2. The word "form" in line 1 is closest in meaning to
    (A) style.
    (B) shape.
    (C) nature.
    (D) design.

3. From the passage, it can be inferred that the Mojave Desert is unusual because
    (A) it is hot even in the shade.
    (B) rain rarely falls there.
    (C) it shelters inactive life.
    (D) very little survives there.

4. The author compares inactive eggs to
    (A) shrimps.
    (B) sand.
    (C) larvae.
    (D) seeds.

5. The word "These" in line 4 refers to
    (A) plants.
    (B) eggs.
    (C) insects.
    (D) fish.

6. According to the passage, the eggs originate
    (A) in the sand.
    (B) on the female.
    (C) in the mud.
    (D) in the lake.

GO ON TO THE NEXT PAGE

7. The word "swarms" in line 7 could best be replaced by
   (A) abounds.
   (B) grows.
   (C) crowd.
   (D) supports.

8. According to the passage, approximately how long does a shrimp live?
   (A) A week
   (B) 12 days
   (C) 13 days
   (D) 14 days plus

9. The word "dormant" in line 19 is closest in meaning to
   (A) dead.
   (B) asleep.
   (C) passive.
   (D) empty.

10. What does the author mean by the phrase "a race against time"?
    (A) The shrimps are in intense competition to reproduce.
    (B) The shrimps must reproduce before the waters recede.
    (C) The shrimps do not have enough time to reproduce.
    (D) Death occurs before the shrimps can reproduce.

Questions 11 - 20

A small but growing group of scholars, evolutionary psychologists, are beginning to sketch the contours of the human mind as designed by natural selection. Some of them even anticipate the coming of a field called "mismatch theory," which would study maladies resulting from contrasts between the modern environment and the "ancestral environment." The one we were designed
5 for. There is no shortage of such maladies to study. Rates of depression have been doubling in some industrial countries roughly every 10 years. Suicide is the third most common cause of death among young adults, after car wrecks and homicides.

   Evolutionary psychology is a long way from explaining all this with precision, but it is already shedding enough light to challenge some conventional wisdom. It suggests, for example, that the
10 nostalgia for the nuclear family of the 1950s is in some way misguided – that the model family of husband at work and wife at home is hardly a "natural" and healthful living arrangement, especially for the wives. Moreover, the bygone lifestyles that do look fairly natural in light of evolutionary psychology appear to have been eroded largely by commercialism. Perhaps the biggest surprise from evolutionary psychology is its depiction of the "animal" in us. Freud, and various thinkers
15 since, saw "civilization" as an oppressive force that thwarts basic animal instincts and urges and transmutes them into psychopathology. However, evolutionary psychology suggests that a larger threat to mental health may be the way civilization thwarts civility. There is a gentler, kinder side of human nature, and it seems increasingly to be a victim of repression in modern society.

11. Which of the following is the main topic of the passage?
    (A) How evolutionary psychology manages modern society
    (B) The problems of illness caused by modern society
    (C) The importance of ancestral environment
    (D) Evolutionary psychologists' views on the nuclear family

12. The word " contours" in line 2 is closest in meaning to
    (A) actions.
    (B) limits.
    (C) structures.
    (D) outlines.

GO ON TO THE NEXT PAGE

13. According to the passage, the death of many young people in industrial countries is mainly caused by
    (A) murder.
    (B) traffic accidents.
    (C) suicide.
    (D) depression.

14. The word "one" in line 4 refers to the
    (A) mismatch theory.
    (B) field.
    (C) modern environment.
    (D) ancestral environment.

15. It can be inferred from the passage that evolutionary psychologists dislike nostalgia for the 1950s because
    (A) it was an unhealthy time to live.
    (B) the nuclear family provided an unsatisfactory lifestyle.
    (C) women who wished to go out to work were misguided.
    (D) family life was seen to be unnatural.

16. The word "bygone" in line 12 could be replaced by
    (A) overlooked.
    (B) forgotten.
    (C) past.
    (D) original.

17. According to the passage, Freud and other psychologists, thought civilization
    (A) showed that people has animal instincts.
    (B) greatly improved people's lives.
    (C) encouraged people to use the basic instincts.
    (D) caused madness in some people.

18. In this passage, the word "civility" in line 17 is closest in meaning to
    (A) courtesy.
    (B) politeness.
    (C) morality.
    (D) formality.

19. In the passage, evolutionary psychologists suggest that in modern society
    (A) victims are always punished.
    (B) peoples' better natures are denied.
    (C) Repressed people are kind and gentle.
    (D) People suffer from repression.

20. Where in the passage does the author suggest a conflict between the ways of living?
    (A) lines 2 - 4
    (B) lines 9 - 12
    (C) lines 13 - 14
    (D) lines 16 - 17

Questions 21 - 30

The history of America could be said to have started in the 600s which saw the beginning of a great tide of emigration from Europe to North America. Spanning more than three centuries, this movement grew from a trickle of a few hundred English colonists to a floodtide of newcomers numbered in the millions. Impelled by powerful and diverse motivations, they built a new
5 civilization on a once savage continent.

The first English immigrants to what is now the United States of America crossed the Atlantic long after thriving Spanish colonies had been established in Mexico, the West Indies, and South America. Like all new travelers to the New World, they came in small, overcrowded ships. During their 6- to 12-week voyages, they lived on meager rations. Many of them died of disease.
10 Ships were often battered by storms, and some were lost at sea.

To the weary voyager, the sight of the American shore brought immense relief. The colonists' first glimpse of the new land was a vista of dense woods. These vast, virgin forests, extending nearly 1,300 miles along the eastern seaboard from north to south, proved to be a treasure house, providing abundant food, fuel, and a rich source of raw
15 materials for houses, furniture, ships, and profitable cargoes for export.

GO ON TO THE NEXT PAGE ➤

The first permanent English settlement in America was a trading post founded in 1607 at Jamestown, in the Old Dominion of Virginia. This region was soon to develop a flourishing economy from its tobacco crop, which found a ready market in England. By 1620, when women were recruited in England to come to Virginia, marry, and make their homes, great plantations had

20 already risen along the James River, and the population had increased to a thousand settlers.

21. The passage mainly discusses American
    (A) civilization.
    (B) exploration.
    (C) immigration.
    (D) agriculture.

22. The word "Spanning" in line 2 is closest in meaning to
    (A) combining.
    (B) reaching.
    (C) uniting.
    (D) bridging.

23. From the passage, it can be inferred that
    (A) most of the immigrants arrived in America in the 1600s.
    (B) emigration to America became more and more popular.
    (C) millions of English people emigrated to America.
    (D) the Spanish were the first to emigrate to America.

24. The word "they" in line 8 refers to
    (A) Spanish colonists.
    (B) Mexican travelers.
    (C) West Indian voyagers.
    (D) English immigrants.

25. It can be inferred from the passage that English immigrants to America often
    (A) were half-starved on their sea voyages.
    (B) died because the voyages were too long.
    (C) traveled in ships which got lost on the voyages.
    (D) were suffering from diseases when they started the voyages.

26. The author refers to the forests as being "virgin" because
    (A) they were completely impenatrable.
    (B) they had never been explored.
    (C) they contained nothing but trees.
    (D) they covered an enormous area.

27. According to the passage, which of the following was welcoming to the exhausted immigrants?
    (A) The shoreline
    (B) Vast woods
    (C) The eastern seaboard
    (D) The settlement

28. The word "which" in line 18 refers to
    (A) region.
    (B) economy.
    (C) crop.
    (D) market.

29. The word "ready" in line 18 could best be replaced by
    (A) waiting.
    (B) perfect.
    (C) chosen.
    (D) total.

30. According to the passage, English women traveled to America to
    (A) become wealthy.
    (B) work on the plantations.
    (C) be employed as housekeepers.
    (D) find a partner.

GO ON TO THE NEXT PAGE

Questions 31 - 40
At the American Association for the Advancement of Science earlier this year, the distinguished entomologist, Professor E. O. Wilson, presented his latest conclusions about the disappearing of some species of life on earth. Based on an estimated total of around 10 million species alive today, and building in all sorts of suitable cautious assumptions, he calculates that the number of
5 species doomed each year is around 27,000. That's 74 a day, 3 an hour. The vast majority of these extinctions is accounted for through the continuous loss of the world's rainforests. Most of the species are entirely unknown and often invisible to the human eye. They are very much at the other end of the scale from the kind of endangered species that most often preoccupy people. Pandas, tigers, elephants, whales: it's no accident that these beautiful and charismatic species so
10 often play the main parts in the drama of today's accelerating extinction.

Organizations like the World Wide Fund for Nature see the complex issues surrounding biodiversity. They know that there may well be many species that are more important than these beautiful animals. However, it's an uphill battle trying to persuade people that an ant can be as crucial as an antelope, a beetle as a bear, let alone generate the necessary momentum to slow the
15 rate of loss. Nevertheless, International Agreements already exist to help protect biodiversity. Some of the most important were signed by 157 countries at the Earth Summit on Biodiversity in Rio Janeiro in 1992.

Two positive trends emerged from the Summit. The first showed the growth in awareness of just how much could be lost by obliterating species before their potential usefulness has been
20 gauged – usefulness in terms of providing genetic material for new drugs, new foods, new fuels, and new products of every kind. Of greater value was the second trend: the ability of science to give a clear answer to the question, "Why does biodiversity matter?" The results of a number of extended experiments which became available in 1995 showed in their conclusions that the more diversity there is, the more productive the ecosystem will be.

31. What is the main idea of the passage?
(A) It is important to have a wide variety of species of life on earth.
(B) Certain small species have more importance than large species.
(C) It is inevitable that all species of life will eventually die out.
(D) Only by biodiversity can all species be preserved permanently.

32. According to the passage, Professor E. O. Wilson thinks the reduction in species is probably due to
(A) a miscalculation in the statistics.
(B) the destruction of natural habitats.
(C) many species being unknown to humans.
(D) humans not being able to see some species.

33. The word "assumptions" in line 4 is closest in meaning to
(A) theories.
(B) principles.
(C) beliefs.
(D) convictions.

34. The word "They" in line 12 refers to
(A) 27,000 species.
(B) charismatic species.
(C) unidentified species.
(D) rainforests.

GO ON TO THE NEXT PAGE

35. What can be inferred from the author's reference to "ants and antelopes" and "beetles and bears"?
    (A) The comparison of sizes of different species is important.
    (B) Irrespective of sizes, all species are valuable.
    (C) The comparison of animal and insect species is absolutely critical.
    (D) All these species are in danger of extinction.

36. In the passage, the phrase "an uphill battle" could be replaced by
    (A) an aggressive action.
    (B) an impossible assignment.
    (C) a lost cause.
    (D) a tough task.

37. According to the passage, after the Earth Summit, a trend appeared which showed
    (A) greater recognition of the possible value of species.
    (B) increasing classification of valuable species.
    (C) growth in supplying companies with genetic material.
    (D) accelerating destruction of certain species.

38. The word "gauged" in line 20 is closest in meaning to
    (A) checked.
    (B) presented.
    (C) planned.
    (D) calculated.

39. The results of the 1995 scientific experiments showed that
    (A) greater diversity produces more dilution.
    (B) greater diversity produces more interaction.
    (C) greater production leads to more deviation.
    (D) greater deviation produces more complexity.

40. From the passage, it can be inferred that the position of life on earth is now
    (A) remaining constant.
    (B) slightly improving.
    (C) rapidly deteriorating.
    (D) constantly changing.

Questions 41 - 50

The song, "Get Your Kicks on Route 66," was written by Bobby Troup as he and wife drove from Chicago to California to start a new life at the end of World War II. The song was recorded by Nat King Cole in 1946, and since then just about every artist from Bing Crosby to the Rolling Stones has followed his example. It has become a Rock 'n' Roll classic, and has
5 transformed the road that it celebrates, Route 66, into a symbol of freedom and adventure. Indeed, it's hard to think of a road that has more instant name recognition. What is more, Route 66, the road to Los Angeles, has a pesonality all of its own. For the novelist, John Steinbeck, it was "The Mother Road," while Woody Guthrie "went walking that ribbon of highway" in another famous song, "This Land is Your Land."

GO ON TO THE NEXT PAGE

10   In spite of its Rock 'n' Roll connections, Route 66 is an old road, completed in 1926. It has seen America change dramatically. In the Great Depression, it was the road of hope that took the unemployed agricultural laborers of Oklahoma out to California in search of work, a phenomenon that was described by John Steinbeck in *The Grapes of Wrath*. In the postwar years, Route 66 was the symbol of optimism and the dream of a better life in California.

15   But the 1950s were to mark the beginning of the end for Route 66, that idyllic decade in American history. The nation's leaders decided that the United States needed a road system that would allow a rapid transportation movement. A Federal Aid Highway Act was thus passed in 1956 and the Interstate Highway System was inaugurated shortly afterwards, and Route 66 was gradually replaced by the Interstates 55, 44, and 50. Today, much of Route 66 still exists
20   physically, but it is mostly back road used by local drivers rather than migrants. The road officially died in 1985 when it was decertified.

41. What is mainly discussed in the passage?
    (A) The loss of importance of a symbolical part of American history.
    (B) The death of Route 66 when songs were no longer written about it.
    (C) The hope that Route 66 offered to migrants.
    (D) The Interstates continuation of the legend of Route 66.

42. The word "his " in line 4 refers to
    (A) Bobby Troup.
    (B) Nat King Cole.
    (C) Bing Crosby.
    (D) The Rolling Stones.

43. According to the passage, all of the following wrote about Route 66 EXCEPT
    (A) Bing Crosby.
    (B) John Steinbeck.
    (C) Bobby Troup.
    (D) Woody Guthrie.

44. The phrase "just about" in line 3 could best be replaced by
    (A) just like.
    (B) at least.
    (C) close to.
    (D) more or less.

45. In the passage, the author implies that Route 66 has a personality because it
    (A) always offered people adventure.
    (B) altered people's point of view.
    (C) presented a better image of America.
    (D) represented the freedom to work.

46. In the passage, the word "ribbon" is closest in meaning to
    (A) banner.
    (B) string.
    (C) track.
    (D) strip.

47. It is implied in the phrase "the beginning of the end" that
    (A) route 66 was deteriorating.
    (B) the 1950s were coming to an end.
    (C) songs about Route 66 were beginning to fade away.
    (D) people were using Route 66 less and less.

48. According to the passage, the Federal Aid Highway Act enabled the authorities to
    (A) upgrade Route 66.
    (B) abandon Route 66.
    (C) supercede Route 66.
    (D) transfer Route 66.

49. The word "thus" in line 17 is closest in meaning to
    (A) moreover.
    (B) usually.
    (C) simply.
    (D) therefore.

50. Where in the passage does the author mention when Route 66 lost its classification
    (A) Lines 5 - 8
    (B) Lines 10 - 11
    (C) Lines 15 - 16
    (D) Lines 20 - 21

THIS IS THE END OF SECTION 3

IF YOU FINISH BEFORE TIME IS CALLED, CHECK YOUR WORK
ON SECTION 3 ONLY.
DO NOT READ OR WORK ON ANY OTHER SECTION OF THE
TEST.

TEST OF WRITTEN ENGLISH ESSAY QUESTION

Time – 30 minutes

Do you agree or disagree with the following statement?

HAPPINESS IS THE ONLY GOAL WORTH PURSUING.

Use reasons and specific examples to support your opinion.

PRACTICE TEST 4

SECTION 1
LISTENING COMPREHENSION

In this section of the test, you will have an opportunity to demonstrate your ability to understand conversations and talks in English. In this section, there are answers to all the questions based on the information heard.

Part A

Directions: In Part A, you will hear short conversations between two people. At the end of each conversation, you will hear a question about the conversation. The conversation and question will not be repeated. Therefore, you must listen carefully to understand what each speaker says. After you hear a question, read the four possible answers in your test book and choose the best answer to the question you heard. Then, on your answer sheet, find the number of the question and fill in the space that corresponds to the letter of the answer you have chosen.

Listen to an example on the recording:

Man: **What seems to be the problem, ma'am?**
Woman: **Well, the light switch is broken and a plug needs repairing.**
Question: **What kind of work does the man probably do?**

In your book you will read: (A) He's a carpenter.
                            (B) He's a plumber.
                            (C) He's an electrician.
                            (D) He's an engineer.

From the conversation, you learn that the light switch is broken and a plug needs repairing. The best answer to the question, "What kind of work does the man probably do?" is *He's an electrician*. Therefore, the correct choice is (C).

Sample Answer
Ⓐ Ⓑ ● Ⓓ

1. (A) Jack was expected to pass his examinations.
    (B) Jack surprised everyone by taking his exam again.
    (C) No one really expected Jack to pass his examinations.
    (D) Jack wasn't expected to fail his exams again.

2. (A) She wants to go
    (B) Parties bore her.
    (C) She's too tired to go.
    (D) Grant bores her.

3. (A) He was feeling sick when he gave his presentation.
    (B) He was interested in presenting his ideas at the front of the class.
    (C) He found it very easy to give a presentation.
    (D) He felt very uncomfortable before the class.

4. (A) Every other hour.
    (B) Every hour and a half.
    (C) Twice an hour.
    (D) Once every hour.

GO ON TO THE NEXT PAGE

5. (A) He last saw Jake at the race track.
   (B) He has no idea where Jake is.
   (C) He's been trying to trace Jake.
   (D) Jake was last seen driving a truck.

6. (A) Persevere for a bit longer.
   (B) Drop the class right away.
   (C) Try and enjoy the class as he did.
   (D) Get ready for the worst part of the class.

7. (A) In a movie theater.
   (B) On the freeway.
   (C) In a shopping mall.
   (D) On a railway train.

8. (A) Sit with the orchestra.
   (B) Try the HOT TIX.
   (C) Go to the matinee.
   (D) Buy orchestra seats.

9. (A) He's not really the best on the team.
   (B) He might do better if he used his head.
   (C) He's become arrogant over his success.
   (D) He's mentally ill.

10. (A) A voter.
    (B) An immigrant.
    (C) A librarian.
    (D) A student.

11. (A) It's better for the woman to apply herself than ask George.
    (B) George knows the procedures better than she does.
    (C) It's no use asking George as he doesn't know what to do.
    (D) With luck, George might know how to apply.

12. (A) He'll go hiking.
    (B) He'll plan his own holiday.
    (C) He won't go away.
    (D) He'll stay in a National Park.

13. (A) He finds reading the newspapers rarely pleasurable.
    (B) He prefers reading the newspaper when he gets the time.
    (C) He enjoys reading fiction, but rarely gets the time.
    (D) He likes reading rare books for pleasure.

14. (A) Yesterday.
    (B) Tuesday.
    (C) Friday.
    (D) Today.

15. (A) The man held on to it tightly.
    (B) He dealt well with the situation.
    (C) He turned it over several times.
    (D) He was certain to have trouble.

16. (A) She would like some help.
    (B) She's not looking for anything special.
    (C) She can't find what she's looking for.
    (D) She doesn't think the man can help her.

17. (A) He thinks Jeremy is as happy as most people.
    (B) He makes as much money as Jeremy.
    (C) He doesn't know if Jeremy is happy with his fortune.
    (D) He thinks Jeremy is happy because he makes a good salary.

18. (A) Employer and worker.
    (B) Doctor and patient.
    (C) Coach and athlete.
    (D) Professor and student.

19. (A) Vote for Ben Hayden.
    (B) Tell a political joke.
    (C) Refuse to cast a ballot in November.
    (D) Vote for another candidate.

GO ON TO THE NEXT PAGE

20. (A) She doesn't know how to register for classes.
    (B) She's on her way to register for her classes.
    (C) She hasn't made up her mind about the classes she wants.
    (D) She doesn't know if she'll register for next summer.

21. (A) Chef and waiter.
    (B) Photographer and model.
    (C) Conductor and musician.
    (D) Dance teacher and student.

22. (A) She agrees the polar bear is more dangerous than the grizzly.
    (B) She doesn't think the grizzly is very fierce.
    (C) She thinks the man doesn't know the real facts about the bears.
    (D) She believes it's true that grizzly and polar bears are mammals.

23. (A) Ernest might do better if he followed her example and increased his lab time.
    (B) She could tutor Ernest in the language lab after school.
    (C) Ernest needs to take another language class after school.
    (D) Ernest spends too much time in the language lab and not enough time in class.

24. (A) The man is just starting his classes.
    (B) The man will have more expenses.
    (C) The man will have to go back to work.
    (D) Now the man has to read the books he bought.

25. (A) Winnie was afraid to catch the flu.
    (B) Winnie wasn't looking forward to her recital.
    (C) Winnie is happy that she hasn't caught the flu.
    (D) Winnie was afraid her recital might be canceled.

26. (A) They had a wonderful time on their way to see Donna.
    (B) They're late because they lost track of time.
    (C) He's sorry they didn't have a good time on their trip.
    (D) They had problems on their way to Donna's.

27. (A) He shouldn't be concerned with the facts.
    (B) She hates math as much as he does.
    (C) She doesn't like the way he talks about his math class.
    (D) Unfortunately, he had to continue taking math classes.

28. (A) At a library.
    (B) At an airport.
    (C) In a newsroom.
    (D) In a lecture hall.

29. (A) Become a member of the man's debating team.
    (B) Join a drama club.
    (C) Stage a protest.
    (D) Step to the podium and tell the truth.

30. (A) Why Bob has been canceling his bowling dates.
    (B) If Bob will cancel a fourth time.
    (C) Whether or not Bob is in trouble.
    (D) If there's any way they can help.

GO ON TO THE NEXT PAGE

Part B

<u>Directions</u>: In this part, you will hear longer conversations. After each conversation, you will be asked several questions. You will hear the conversations and the questions about them only one time. They will not be repeated. Therefore, you must listen carefully to understand what each speaker says.

After you hear a question, read the four possible answers in your test book and choose which <u>one</u> is the best answer to the question you heard. Then, on your answer sheet, find the number of the question and fill in the space that corresponds to the letter of the answer you have chosen.

Remember, you should not take notes or write on your test paper.

31. (A) Restaurant owner.
    (B) Social consultant.
    (C) College professor.
    (D) Business executive.

32. (A) The brother and sister-in-law of the woman.
    (B) The woman's parents.
    (C) The woman's own.
    (D) The man's.

33. (A) Take in a show and eat out.
    (B) Have a dinner party.
    (C) Go to a fancy concert.
    (D) Go to a restaurant with music.

34. (A) She has a good chance.
    (B) It's something he wouldn't try to do.
    (C) She should try to do something.
    (D) She is going to be surprised.

35. (A) In a classroom.
    (B) In a laboratory.
    (C) In a restaurant.
    (D) In a studio.

36. (A) He is late for an appointment.
    (B) He is working too hard.
    (C) He never finishes what he starts.
    (D) He needs to study harder.

37. (A) Become well known for his art.
    (B) Take a break from his work.
    (C) Develop a new technique.
    (D) Leave his latest piece unfinished.

38. (A) She thinks it will make him famous.
    (B) She thinks it's fascinating.
    (C) She doesn't really like it.
    (D) She thinks he needs to smooth the edges.

GO ON TO THE NEXT PAGE

Part C

Directions: In this part, you will hear various talks. After each talk, you will be asked several questions. The talks and questions will not be repeated. They will not be written out for you. Therefore, you must listen carefully to understand what the speaker says.

   After you hear a question, read the four possible answers in your test book and choose which one is the best answer to the question you heard. Then, on your answer sheet, find the number of the question and fill in the space that corresponds to the letter of the answer you have chosen.

Listen to this sample talk.
You will hear: **The National Health Research Center, perhaps more than any other organization, will directly affect the lives of millions of Americans every day. The Health Research Center volunteers will work all over the United States to provide information on diet and lifestyles. The bulk of the foundation's time will be spent conducting seminars and distributing pamphlets on how to prevent major illness and increase longevity. A free long-distance 800 number is available for anyone with health-related questions.**

Now listen to the following question.

What is the speaker's purpose?

You will read: (A) To get you to join the foundation.
                (B) To inform you of the existence of the Health Research Center.
                (C) To persuade you to give a donation to the foundation.
                (D) To ask you to distribute pamphlets for the foundation.

The best answer to the question, "What is the speaker's purpose?" is *To inform you of the existence of the Health Research Center.* Therefore, you should choose answer (B).

Sample Answer
(A) ● (C) (D)

Now listen to the next example.

Why would you use the center's 800 number?

You will read: (A) To volunteer to distribute pamphlets.
                (B) To make a contribution to the Health Research Center.
                (C) To obtain a schedule of seminars.
                (D) To ask questions regarding good health.

The best answer to the question, "Why would you use the center's 800 number?" is *To ask questions regarding good health.* Therefore, you should choose answer (D).

Sample Answer
(A) (B) (C) ●

GO ON TO THE NEXT PAGE

39. (A) To describe the physical characteristics of Mars.
    (B) To compare Mars with Earth.
    (C) To convince doubters of the impossibility of life on Mars.
    (D) To prepare people for the exploration of Mars.

40. (A) Physics.
    (B) Astronomy.
    (C) Anthropology.
    (D) Civil Engineering.

41. (A) It has a reddish color.
    (B) It is the brightest.
    (C) It is the closest to Earth.
    (D) It has two small moons.

42. (A) Seasons.
    (B) Polar ice caps.
    (C) Clouds.
    (D) Oxygen.

43. (A) Mars has already been explored to its fullest extent.
    (B) Mars may have some form of intelligent life.
    (C) A manned expedition to Mars is being planned.
    (D) The name "Red Planet" is not appropriate for Mars.

44. (A) How milk chocolate is made.
    (B) How the Spanish explorers brought chocolate to Europe.
    (C) The history of chocolate.
    (D) The growing popularity of chocolate.

45. (A) Europe.
    (B) South America.
    (C) Spain.
    (D) England.

46. (A) Improve the smoothness of chocolate.
    (B) Improve the taste of chocolate.
    (C) Combine chocolate with cheese.
    (D) Mix chocolate with milk.

47. (A) It is sweeter.
    (B) It is smoother.
    (C) It is thicker.
    (D) It has more raw chocolate in it.

48. (A) To entertain the people waiting to join the tour.
    (B) To persuade the audience to join the tour.
    (C) To inform the audience of what they can expect of the tour.
    (D) To get the audience to spend money during the tour.

49. (A) Beside the shop.
    (B) Behind the back lot.
    (C) Near the kiosk.
    (D) At the restaurant.

50. (A) Enthusiastic.
    (B) Indifferent.
    (C) Irritated.
    (D) Concerned.

THIS IS THE END OF THE LISTENING COMPREHENSION SECTION OF THE TEST

THE NEXT PART OF THE TEST IS SECTION 2.
TURN TO THE DIRECTIONS FOR SECTION 2 IN YOUR TEST BOOK.
READ THEM AND BEGIN WORK.
DO NOT READ OR WORK ON ANY OTHER SECTION OF THE TEST.

SECTION 2
STRUCTURE AND WRITTEN EXPRESSION

Time – 25 minutes

This section is designed to measure your ability to recognize language that is appropriate for standard written English. There are two types of questions in this section, with special directions for each type.

<u>Directions:</u> Questions 1-15 are incomplete sentences. Beneath each sentence you will see four words or phrases, marked (A), (B), (C), and (D). Choose the <u>one</u> word or phrase that best completes the sentence. Then, on your answer sheet, find the number of the question and fill in the space that corresponds to the letter of the answer you have chosen. Fill in the space so that the letter inside the oval cannot be seen.

Example I

    Sound comes in waves, and the
    higher the frequency, ...
    (A) higher is the pitch.
    (B) the pitch is higher.
    (C) the higher the pitch.
    (D) pitch is the higher.

The sentence should read, "Sound comes in waves, and the higher the frequency, the higher the pitch." Therefore, you should choose answer (C).

Example II

    Fire safety in family houses, ...
    most fire deaths occur, is difficult
    to achieve.
    (A) where
    (B) why
    (C) how
    (D) when

<u>Sample Answer</u>
Ⓐ Ⓑ ● Ⓓ

The sentence should read, "Fire safety in family houses, where most fire deaths occur, is difficult to achieve." Therefore, you should choose answer (A).

After you read the directions, begin work on the questions.

<u>Sample Answer</u>
● Ⓑ Ⓒ Ⓓ

1. Water . . . . . one of the few substances that expand upon freezing.
   (A) it is
   (B) being
   (C) which is
   (D) is

2. . . . . . , sewing had been done by boring a hole with a bone, and then passing a fiber through the opening.
   (A) Before the invention of the needle
   (B) With the invention of the needle
   (C) It was during the needle's invention
   (D) After the needle's invention

3. The name Canada is derived from the Iroquoian Indian word "Kanata", ... a village or community.
   (A) means
   (B) meaning
   (C) it means
   (D) to mean

4. . . . . . is the major method used by the body to dispose of excess heat and maintain a normal body temperature.
   (A) That evaporation
   (B) The evaporation
   (C) Evaporation
   (D) While evaporation

5. The cattle kingdom of the Great Plains had a brief but . . . . . from 1865 to 1885.
   (A) brilliant existence
   (B) was a brilliant existence
   (C) had existed brilliantly
   (D) brilliantly existed

6. . . . . . the moon has no water, its solid crust does respond to the gravitational force of the earth.
   (A) Although
   (B) However
   (C) Therefore
   (D) Except

7. Mark Twain, one of the greatest American novelists, began his career on a newspaper and . . . . . to be a journalist.
   (A) himself long considered
   (B) long considered himself
   (C) long considering himself
   (D) was long himself considered

8. . . . . . , it is widely used in making flares and fireworks.
   (A) Burning magnesium produces a brilliant white light
   (B) As the brilliant white light that burning magnesium produces
   (C) The brilliant white light of burning magnesium
   (D) Because of the brilliant white light of magnesium

9. Mutual harm plays a large part in the animal world not only between members of the same species . . . . .
   (A) but only between members of the same society.
   (B) but even between members of the same society.
   (C) and also between members of the same society.
   (D) as well as between members of the same society.

10. . . . . . , 70 percent alcohol is more effective than 100 percent alcohol.
    (A) An antiseptic used
    (B) When used as an antiseptic
    (C) An antiseptic when used
    (D) How an antiseptic is used

GO ON TO THE NEXT PAGE ▶

11. The most spectacular recurring comet to be seen in historic times . . . . . , named after the English astronomer Edmund Halley, who discovered its periodicity in 1705.
    (A) is probably Halley's Comet
    (B) that is probably Halley's Comet
    (C) Most probably Halley's Comet
    (D) Halley's Comet

12. . . . . . that the Americas were populated through Alaska by small groups of Siberian hunters who crossed the Bering Strait.
    (A) The majority of anthropologists believing
    (B) Believed by the majority of anthropologists
    (C) With the majority of anthropologists believing
    (D) The majority of anthropologists believe

13. In the 1790s, Oliver Evans invented a card-making machine, constructed an automatic flour mill, ... , and combined theory and practice in America's first textbook on mechanical engineering.
    (A) has made improvements upon the steam engine
    (B) improved upon the steam engine
    (C) improving upon the steam engine
    (D) the improvement of the steam engine

14. The sun, ... , radiates an amount of power equal to about a million billion billion kilowatts.
    (A) is a typical star
    (B) typical star
    (C) as a typical star
    (D) for a typical star

15. Hydrocarbons, ... by engine exhausts, react with nitrogen oxides in the presence of sunlight to form complex toxic gases.
    (A) are given off
    (B) given off
    (C) give off
    (D) they are given off

GO ON TO THE NEXT PAGE

<u>Directions:</u> Questions 16-40 each sentence had four underlined words or phrases. The four underlined parts of the sentence are marked (A), (B), (C), and (D). Identify the <u>one</u> underlined word or phrase that must be changed in order for the sentence to be correct. Then, on your answer sheet, find the number of the question and fill in the space that corresponds to the letter of the answer you have chosen.

Example I

    After Newton <u>has observed</u> an apple <u>fall</u>
                A   B
    to the ground, he formulated <u>the</u> law of
                                  C

    <u>gravity</u>.
      D

The underlined words <u>has observed</u> would not be acceptable in carefully written English. The past perfect form of the verb should be used to express the first of two completed actions in the past. Therefore, the sentence should read, "After Newton had observed an apple fall to the ground, he formulated the law of gravity." To answer the question correctly, you should choose (A).

<u>Sample Answer</u>
● Ⓑ Ⓒ Ⓓ

Example II

    In 1740, John Newbery was <u>the</u>
                            A
    first publisher <u>to produce</u>
                 B
    books <u>which</u> children really
           C
    wanted <u>read</u>.
          D

The underlined word <u>read</u> would not be accepted in carefully written English. The infinitive form to read should be used because the verb wanted takes an infinitive with "to." Therefore, the sentence should read, "In 1740, John Newbery was the first publisher to produce books which children really wanted to read." To answer the question correctly, you should choose (D).

<u>Sample Answer</u>
Ⓐ Ⓑ Ⓒ ●

After you read the directions, begin work on the questions.

GO ON TO THE NEXT PAGE ➤

16. Alike oxygen, which is chemically changed by our bodies into carbon dioxide, nitrogen is
    A   B
    merely exhaled back into the air.
    C   D

17. Rattlesnakes feed only on warm-blood animals; the eastern diamond-back, for instance, feeds
                           A   B
    almost exclusively on cottontail rabbits.
           C   D

18. The Mississippi Delta have been growing and moving south for many millions of years.
                         A   B   C   D

19. Hunger depends of the blood's concentration of glucose, a kind of sugar.
             A B   C   D

20. The first official use of the title "The United States of America" occurred in Declaration of
    A   B   C   D
    Independence in 1776.

21. Whenever the wind blows from the ocean toward the land, the ocean exerts a moderate effect
                     A   B   C   D
    on the temperature of the land.

22. In 1846, Richard Hoe invented the steam cylinder rotary press, making them possible to print
                                                     A   B   C
    newspapers at a much faster rate and a much lower cost.
                                      D

23. Cancer cells are often moved from original sites to other part of the body by the blood and
    A   B   C   D
    lymph.

24. The chance of lightning striking a building depend on its height.
    A   B   C D

25. The United States has seen a shift from small farms that grew a wide range of crops to large
                      A   B
    farms that engaging in monoculture – the intensive production of single crops.
               C   D

26. Ink blot testing was invented by psychiatrist Hermann Rorschach as a tool to ferret out of
                     A   B
    a person unconscious mind various bits and pieces of information.
    C   D

27. Encephalitis, a disease present in the United States, are transmitted to people by birds and
                            A   B   C   D
    mosquitoes.

GO ON TO THE NEXT PAGE

28. The 1890s <u>saw</u> <u>the birth</u> <u>of</u> the bicycle <u>crazy</u> in the Unites States.
           A   B   C   D

29. The name Albert Einstein <u>has become</u> synonymous with his theory of <u>relative</u> <u>in the minds</u> of
                               A   B   C

    most scientists and <u>laymen</u>.
                        D

30. <u>One</u> geothermal field in California, the Imperial Valley, <u>it</u> extends for <u>some</u> 2,000 miles and
 A   B   C

    contains water <u>heated</u> as high as 700°F.
                   D

31. The United Nations <u>was</u> <u>officially</u> established on October 24, 1945, and originally had 51
                         A   B

    <u>members</u> <u>nations</u>.
    C   D

32. Coral atolls, those <u>ring-shaped</u> islands that <u>surround</u> a lagoon, are <u>made up of</u> the skeletons
                 A   B   C

    of <u>numerable</u> marine animals.
       D

33. Noah Webster's *American Spelling Book* (1783), <u>commonly known</u> as "the blue-backed
                                       A

    speller," <u>eventua</u>l sold over 100 million copies to become <u>the best selling book</u> in the entire
        B   C

    history of American <u>publishing</u>.
          D

34. The hydra is a fresh-water animal about half an inch <u>long</u> that <u>goes</u> places <u>on</u> turning
                                    A   B   C

    somersaults <u>on its</u> tentacles.
          D

35. The American <u>bald</u> eagle was chosen as the emblem of the United States because it <u>is native</u>
          A   B

    to North America and <u>symbolizes</u> strength, <u>vigil</u>, and courage.
                    C   D

36. New York opened <u>its</u> first <u>elevated</u> railway in 1870, and in 1897, Boston <u>put</u> the streetcars
                 A   B   C

    underground, <u>completed</u> the first American subway.
          D

GO ON TO THE NEXT PAGE ➤

37. Birds and bats <u>can hear</u> the sounds made by insects and distinguish between desirable and
                A

    undesirable <u>species</u> by the number of wing beats per second <u>that</u> each makes <u>itself</u>.
            B   C   D

38. The <u>most great</u> trumpet player, Louis Armstrong, went from New Orleans to Chicago in 1922
            A

    to join a band that helped <u>spread</u> jazz <u>through</u> phonograph <u>recordings</u>.
                               B   C   D

39. Chinooks are warm, dry winds <u>that</u> often <u>cause</u> a temperature <u>rising</u> of 20°F to 40°F in 15
                                    A   B   C

    minutes <u>or less</u>.
             D

40. Magnesium <u>forms</u> a tough surface <u>coating</u> <u>it</u> protects the <u>underlying</u> metal from tarnishing.
            A   B C   D

THIS IS THE END OF SECTION 2

IF YOU FINISH BEFORE TIME IS CALLED, CHECK YOUR WORK
ON SECTION 2 ONLY.
DO NOT READ OR WORK ON ANY OTHER SECTION OF THE
TEST.
THE SUPERVISOR WILL TELL YOU WHEN TO BEGIN WORK ON
SECTION 3.

SECTION 3
READING COMPREHENSION

Time – 55 minutes

This section is designed to measure your comprehension of standard written English.

<u>Directions:</u> In this section, you will read several passages. Each is followed by a number of questions about it. For questions 1-50, you are to choose the <u>one</u> best answer, (A), (B), (C), or (D), to each question. Then on your answer sheet, find the number of the question and fill in the space that corresponds to the letter of the answer you have chosen.

Answer all questions about the information in a passage on the basis of what is <u>stated</u> or <u>implied</u> in that passage.

Read the following passage:

The Mediterranean fruit fly is one of the world's most destructive insect pests. It attacks more than 250 kinds of fruits, nuts, and vegetables. If the pest made its way into fruit and vegetable-growing parts of the United States, supplies of produce would go down and prices would go up. It would devastate commercial agriculture and could cost consumers an estimated additional $820
5 million per year.

Example I

    What is the main idea of the passage?
    (A) Farmers need to produce more as a result of the Medfly.
    (B) Commercial agriculture is very expensive in the United States.
    (C) People should be aware of the danger of the Medfly.
    (D) Many fruits and vegetables are infested by the Medfly in the United States.

The main idea of the passage is to warn people about the danger of the Medfly. Therefore, you should choose answer (C).

Sample Answer
Ⓐ   Ⓑ   ●   Ⓓ

Example II

    In line 3, the word "It" refers to
    (A) commercial agriculture.
    (B) supplies of produce.
    (C) The Mediterranean fruit fly.
    (D) $820 million.

The word "It" refers to "if the pest made its way," the pest is the Medfly, so you should choose answer (C).

Sample Answer
Ⓐ   Ⓑ   ●   Ⓓ

Now begin work on the questions.

GO ON TO THE NEXT PAGE

3 • 3 • 3 • 3 • 3 • 3 • 3

Questions 1 -10

The air above our head is becoming cleaner. A breath of fresh air has been running right round the planet for the past five years. The planet is apparently purging itself of pollution. Paul Novell of the University of Colorado, the co-author of a report on this phenomenon says, "It seems as if the planet's own cleansing service has suddenly got a new lease of life. Suddenly, there are a lot
5 of changes going on up there."

Estimates of the death toll from urban smogs have been steadily rising, so the new cleaner trend could have significant consequences for life expectancy in cities as well as for the planet itself. The sudden and unexpected reversal of several decades of worsening pollution extends from the air in city streets to the remotest mid-Pacific Ocean and Antartica.
10 Among the pollutants which have begun to disappear from the atmosphere are carbon monoxide, from car exhausts and burning rain forests, and methane from the guts of cattle, paddy fields, and gas fields. Even carbon dioxide, the main gas behind global warming, has fallen slightly.

There are two theories about why pollution is disappearing. First, that there is less pollution to start with due to laws to cut down urban smogs and acid rain starting to have a global impact.
15 Second, that the planet may be becoming more efficient at cleaning up.

The main planetary clean-up agent is a chemical called hydroxyl. It is present throughout the atmosphere in tiny quantities and removes most pollutants from the air by oxidizing them. The amount of hydroxyl in the air had fallen by a quarter in the 1980s. Now, it may be reviving for two reasons: ironically, because the ozone hole has expanded, letting in more ultraviolet radiation
20 into the lower atmosphere, where it manufactures hydroxyl. Then the stricter controls on vehicle exhausts in America and Europe may have cut global carbon monoxide emissions, thereby allowing more hydroxyl to clean up other pollutants.

1. What is the main topic of the passage?
   (A) The decreasing pollution of the atmosphere
   (B) The changing pollutants in the atmosphere
   (C) Hydroxyl's influence on the atmosphere
   (D) The oxygenation of the atmosphere

2. The word "purging" in line 2 is closest in meaning to
   (A) destroying.
   (B) refining.
   (C) filtering.
   (D) ridding.

3. According to the passage, life expectancy partly depends on people having
   (A) access to details about atmospheric pollution.
   (B) recommendations from university research.
   (C) improvement in atmospheric conditions.
   (D) changes in their lifestyle.

4. The word "toll" in line 6 could best be replaced by
   (A) costs.
   (B) count.
   (C) damage.
   (D) loss.

5. What does the author suggest is the main cause of pollution reduction?
   (A) Less impact from burning forests
   (B) A smaller number of cars
   (C) A curtailment of chemicals
   (D) Fewer cattle and gas fields

6. The word "It" in line 16 refers to
   (A) urban smog.
   (B) a clean-up agent.
   (C) acid rain.
   (D) the ozone hole.

GO ON TO THE NEXT PAGE

7. It can be inferred from the passage that the cleansing of the planet is
   (A) inexplicable.
   (B) confusing.
   (C) surprising.
   (D) predictable.

8. Based on information in the passage, all of the following information referring to hydroxyl is true EXCEPT
   (A) the reduction in the ozone layer is beneficial to hydroxyl.
   (B) Oxydization of pollutants is carried out by hydroxyl.
   (C) there is difficulty in destroying carbon dioxide by hydroxyl.
   (D) ultraviolet radiation increases production of hydroxyl.

9. The word "reviving" in line 18 is closest in meaning to
   (A) reappearing.
   (B) refreshing.
   (C) reproducing.
   (D) repeating.

10. The passage supports which of the following conclusions?
   (A) The decrease of methane has enabled ultraviolet radiation to enter the atmosphere.
   (B) An expansion in hydroxyl has enlarged the ozone hole.
   (C) The reduction in carbon dioxide has produced a cleaner atmosphere.
   (D) The beneficial effect of hydroxyl has aided the cleansing process.

Questions 11 - 20

Psychodrama was introduced into the United States in 1925, and since then a number of clinical methods have developed: the therapeutic psychodrama, the sociodrama, role playing, analytic psychodrama, and various modifications of them.

The chief participants in a therapeutic psychodrama are the protagonist, or patient; the director,
5 or chief therapist; the auxiliary egos, or other patient-actors; and the group. The protagonist presents either a private or a group problem; the auxiliary egos help him to bring his personal and collective drama to life and to correct it. Meaningful psychological experiences of the protagonist are given shape more thoroughly and more completely than life would permit under normal circumstances. A psychodrama can be produced anywhere, wherever patients find themselves, in
10 a private home, a hospital, a schoolroom, or a military barracks. It sets up its "laboratory" everywhere. Most advantageous is a specially adapted therapeutic space containing a stage. Psychodrama is either protagonist-centered (the private problem of the protagonist) or group-centered (the problem of the group). In general, it is important that the theme, whether it is private or collective, be a truly experienced problem of the participants (real or symbolic). The
15 participants should represent their experiences spontaneously, although the repetition of a theme can frequently be of therapeutic advantage. Next to the protagonist, the auxiliary egos and the chief therapist play an important part. It is their responsibility to bring the therapeutic productivity of the group to as high a level as possible.

The protagonist, in order to get into the production, must be motivated consciously or
20 unconsciously. The motive may be, among other things, self-realization, relief from mental anguish, ability to function in a social group. He is frustrated, let us say, in the role of father or any other role in life itself, and he enjoys the mastery and realization by means of psychodrama which gives him symbolic satisfaction.

GO ON TO THE NEXT PAGE

11. What does the passage mainly discuss?
    (A) How patients can gain satisfaction by writing plays about their lives
    (B) How psychodrama can help resolve emotional conflicts
    (C) How actors can gain self-understanding by considering other people's problems
    (D) How important it is for patients and therapists to act together

12. The word "modifications" in line 3 is closest in meaning to
    (A) comparisons.
    (B) categories.
    (C) alterations.
    (D) classifications.

13. According to the passage, psychodrama enables patients to
    (A) become actors.
    (B) produce a play.
    (C) have new experiences.
    (D) unlock their conflicts.

14. The word "It" in line 10 refers to
    (A) laboratory.
    (B) psychodrama.
    (C) hospital.
    (D) stage.

15. What is the role of the auxiliary egos in psychodramas?
    (A) To help the protagonists act better
    (B) To criticise the protagonist's behavior
    (C) To assist the protagonists to resolve their problems
    (D) To make the protagonist feel more important

16. What is the author implying by the use of the word "laboratory" in line 10?
    (A) That people with psychological problems have to be dealt with in a special place
    (B) That psychological problems are analyzed in a controlled setting
    (C) That people's problems have to be dealt with in a scientific way
    (D) That therapists control people in experiment settings

17. It can be inferred from the passage that psychodrama is beneficial as it
    (A) encourages people to explore their subconscious motives.
    (B) relieves the protagonist from having to think too much.
    (C) allows the patients to have experiences of anxiety.
    (D) presents patients with the deepest problems.

18. The phrase "let us say" in line 21 could best be replaced by
    (A) therefore.
    (B) for example.
    (C) in this way.
    (D) of course.

19. For which of the following terms does the author provide a definition?
    (A) Theme
    (B) Laboratory
    (C) Motive
    (D) Space

20. Where in the passage does the author suggest that a patient may be suffering from anxiety?
    (A) Lines 5 - 7
    (B) Lines 7 - 10
    (C) Lines 14 - 16
    (D) Lines 20 - 21

GO ON TO THE NEXT PAGE

Questions 21 - 30

As the Millennium approaches, an economic earthquake is shaking the globe, producing an upheaval comparable to the Industrial Revolution that gave birth to the manufacturing age. The Information Revolution is powered by breathtaking technological advances, accelerating world trade and the spread of free-market policies. Economic values are being torn down. Vast new
5 markets beckon. Ten years ago, the free-market economies encompassed 1 billion people. Now, says U.S. Treasury Under Secretary Lawrence Summers, "It is only a slight exaggeration to say this is the era when 3 billion people entered the free-market."

Yet the world is also entering an era of uncertainty and dislocation. Just as the Industrial Revolution unleashed forces that destroyed the old agricultural order, so the Information
10 Revolution is creating a new global division of labor with far-reaching consequences for the fortunes of nations and individuals.

The only certainty, perhaps, is the size and speed of change. The globalized economy is one of 24-hour financial markets, huge split-second flows of international funds, and intense competition as companies roam the world for capital, labor, technology, raw materials, and markets. More
15 flexible production techniques are allowing giant global corporations to locate their activities wherever it is economically most advantageous. The traditional "industrial" countries, led by the U.S., are moving inexorably, though at differing speeds, to service-based economies. In the not to distant future, only 1 in 10 of their workers will be employed in manufacturing.

Many economists are confident that a bright era of world growth will emerge from the current
20 disruptions, that the changes are no more disturbing than the 18th century moves from countryside to industry. Service jobs replacing those in manufacturing are by no means all low paid. They include banking, insurance, marketing, design, and computer programming.

21. Which of the following is the main topic of the passage?
    (A) The changing job market
    (B) Changing financial markets
    (C) Global increase in employment
    (D) Worldwide economic changes

22. The word "upheaval" in line 2 is closest in meaning to
    (A) convulsion.
    (B) revolution.
    (C) agitation.
    (D) explosion.

23. It can be inferred from the passage that there will be more
    (A) manufacturing in the future.
    (B) global trade.
    (C) people employed in manufacturing.
    (D) free-lance workers.

24. The author compares the Information Revolution to
    (A) free-market economies.
    (B) the manufacturing age.
    (C) the Industrial Revolution.
    (D) an economic age.

25. The word "unleashed" in line 9 could best be replaced by
    (A) separated.
    (B) liberated.
    (C) justified.
    (D) divided.

26. According to the passage, the globalized economy helps to
    (A) increase competitiveness.
    (B) cause corporate uncertainty.
    (C) develop world travel.
    (D) produce large companies.

GO ON TO THE NEXT PAGE

27. It can be inferred from the passage that the Information Revolution will
    (A) produce more industries.
    (B) help destroy manufacturing.
    (C) increase the speed of change.
    (D) create new jobs.

28. The word "roam" in line 14 is closest in meaning to
    (A) walk.
    (B) cross.
    (C) travel.
    (D) discover.

29. The word "they" in line 22 refers to
    (A) economists.
    (B) jobs.
    (C) changes.
    (D) moves.

30. Where does the author mention the economy in connection with employment?
    (A) Lines 1 - 2
    (B) Lines 5 - 8
    (C) Lines 8 - 11
    (D) Lines 21 - 22

Questions 31 - 40

Stickleback fish use sign stimuli in their systems of behavior. At the breeding season, the male develops a red underside which acts as a deterrent to other males which swim near. If the intruder persists, it will be attacked and driven off. Niko Tinbergen, the animal behaviorist, noticed that the whole process of reproduction in the stickleback could be seen as a series of reactions to sign
5 stimuli, each one triggering off the next.
      Once its territory is secure, the male stickleback constructs a nest. It makes a shallow pit in the sand, collects small pieces of wood, and glues them together by means of a sticky secretion. It then forces its way through the nest, so molding it into the shape of a tunnel. If a female swims near, her bulging abdomen (due to the eggs inside) stimulates the male to perform a zig-zag dance
10 around her, thus displaying his red underside. If the female is ready to lay, she responds by curving her head and tail upwards. This behavior excites the male who swims to the nest, causing her to follow. He then prods the entrance with his snout, stimulating the female to push past him and go inside. The sight of the female's projecting tail stimulates the male to thrust at it. This causes her to lay. When she swims off, he enters and fertilizes the eggs. The male then guards the young, and
15 if they stray, sucks them into his mouth and spits them back into the nest.
      Sign stimuli behavior such as this is not learned, and in some way not understood, but is innate, passed from one generation to the next instinctively.

31. What does the passage mainly discuss?
    (A) Territorial rights of sticklebacks
    (B) Reproductive systems of sticklebacks
    (C) Communicative methods of sticklebacks
    (D) Behavioral patterns of sticklebacks

32. The word "deterrent" in line 2 is closest in meaning to
    (A) defense.
    (B) warning.
    (C) protest.
    (D) restraint.

33. According to the passage, reproduction in sticklebacks is triggered by the male
    (A) fighting a rival.
    (B) building a nest.
    (C) changing color.
    (D) making a pit.

34. The word "it" in line 8 refers to
    (A) stickleback.
    (B) secretion.
    (C) glue.
    (D) sand.

GO ON TO THE NEXT PAGE

35. In lines 6-7, the author mentions male sticklebacks as examples of fish that
    (A) build fish-shaped nests.
    (B) live mainly in tunnels.
    (C) breed at the bottom of the sea.
    (D) glue sand to wood for nests.

36. The word "bulging" in line 9 could best be replaced by
    (A) lumpy.
    (B) bulky.
    (C) fleshy.
    (D) swollen.

37. It can be inferred from the passage that the main incentive for the female to lay eggs is
    (A) watching the male dancer.
    (B) entering the nest.
    (C) seeing the male's underside.
    (D) being touched by the male.

38. According to the passage, the young fish can be harmed by
    (A) lacking oxygen.
    (B) getting cold.
    (C) becoming hot.
    (D) being swallowed.

39. The word "stray" in line 15 is closest in meaning to
    (A) disappear.
    (B) escape.
    (C) survive.
    (D) hide.

40. According to the passage, sign stimuli to sticklebacks are
    (A) misunderstood.
    (B) automatic.
    (C) unrecognisable.
    (D) forgetable.

GO ON TO THE NEXT PAGE

Questions 41 - 50

In the exploration of the linguistic life cycle, it is apparent that is is much more difficult to learn a second language in adulthood than a first language in childhood. Most adults never completely master a foreign language, especially in phonology – hence the ubiquitous foreign accent. Their development often "fossilizes" into permanent error patterns that no teaching or correction can
5 undo. Of course, there are great individual differences, which depend on effort, attitudes, amount of exposure, quality of teaching, and plain talent, but there seems to be a cap for the best adults in the best circumstances.

Many explanations have been advanced for children's superiority: they exploit Motherese (the simplified, repetitive conversation between parents and children), make errors unself-consciously,
10 are more motivated to communicate, like to conform, are not set in their ways, and have no first language to interfere. But some of these accounts are unlikely, based on what is known about how language acquisition works. Recent evidence is calling these social and motivation explanations into doubt. Holding every other factor constant, a key factor stands out: sheer age.

Systematic evidence comes from the psychologist Elissa Newport and her colleagues. They
15 tested Korean and Chinese-born students at the University of Illinois who had spent at least ten years in the United States. The immigrants were given a list of 276 simple English sentences, half of them containing some grammatical error. The immigrants who came to the United States between the ages of 3 and 7 performed identically to American-born students. Those who arrived between the ages of 8 and 15 did worse the later they arrived, and those who arrived between 17
20 and 39 did the worst of all, and showed huge variability unrelated to their age of arrival.

41. The passage mainly discusses
(A) adult differences in learning a foreign language.
(B) children's ability to learn a language.
(C) the age factor in learning languages fast.
(D) research into language acquisition.

42. From the passage, it can be inferred that "phonology" is the study of
(A) the grammar of a language.
(B) the rules of a language.
(C) the vocabulary of a language.
(D) the sound system of a language.

43. The word "cap" in line 6 is closest in meaning to
(A) prize.
(B) limit.
(C) covering.
(D) level.

44. According to the passage, young children learn languages quickly for all of the following reasons EXCEPT
(A) they make many mistakes.
(B) they want to talk.
(C) their approach is flexible.
(D) they frequently repeat words.

45. The word "set" in line 10 could best be replaced by
(A) fixed.
(B) changed.
(C) stable.
(D) formed.

46. The word "unrelated" in line 20 is closest in meaning to
(A) unconnected.
(B) unfamiliar.
(C) unclassified.
(D) unidentified.

GO ON TO THE NEXT PAGE

47. In the experiment in the passage, the psychologists discovered
    (A) most students had lived in the U.S. for more than 10 years.
    (B) older students were unable to learn English.
    (C) young students learned English best.
    (D) students who arrived late were worst of all.

48. The word "who" in line 15 refers to
    (A) Elissa Newport.
    (B) Koreans.
    (C) students.
    (D) colleagues.

49. According to the passage, what was the purpose of examining a sample number of immigrants?
    (A) To compare different age groups
    (B) To detect differences in nationalities
    (C) To confirm different language characteristics
    (D) To measure the use of grammar

50. Where in the passage does the author mention that children acquire their own language easily?
    (A) Lines 1 - 2
    (B) Lines 8 - 11
    (C) Lines 14 - 16
    (D) Lines 17 - 18

THIS IS THE END OF SECTION 3

IF YOU FINISH BEFORE TIME IS CALLED, CHECK YOUR WORK
ON SECTION 3 ONLY.
DO NOT READ OR WORK ON ANY OTHER SECTION OF THE
TEST.

TEST OF WRITTEN ENGLISH ESSAY QUESTION

Time – 30 minutes

INVENTIONS SUCH AS THE BICYCLE AND THE TELEPHONE HAVE
HAD IMPORTANT EFFECTS ON OUR LIVES.

Choose another invention that you think is important.

Give specific reasons for your choice.

PRACTICE TEST 5

SECTION 1
LISTENING COMPREHENSION

In this section of the test, you will have an opportunity to demonstrate your ability to understand conversations and talks in English. In this section, there are answers to all the questions based on the information heard.

Part A

<u>Directions:</u> In Part A, you will hear short conversations between two people. At the end of each conversation, you will hear a question about the conversation. The conversation and question will not be repeated. Therefore, you must listen carefully to understand what each speaker says. After you hear a question, read the four possible answers in your test book and choose the best answer to the question you heard. Then, on your answer sheet, find the number of the question and fill in the space that corresponds to the letter of the answer you have chosen.

Listen to an example on the recording:

      Man: **What seems to be the problem, ma'am?**
      Woman: **Well, the light switch is broken and a plug needs repairing.**
      Question: **What kind of work does the man probably do?**

In your book you will read: (A) He's a carpenter.
                            (B) He's a plumber.
                            (C) He's an electrician.
                            (D) He's an engineer.

From the conversation, you learn that the light switch is broken and a plug needs repairing. The best answer to the question, "What kind of work does the man probably do?" is *He's an electrician.* Therefore, the correct choice is (C).

<u>Sample Answer</u>
Ⓐ Ⓑ ● Ⓓ

1. (A) In a restaurant.
   (B) In a cafeteria.
   (C) In a hotel lobby.
   (D) At the airport check-in.

2. (A) He would like to meet her in the snack bar in the afternoon.
   (B) He thinks they should meet at noon in the snack bar.
   (C) He would like a snack at the bar first.
   (D) He does not think that the snack bar is a good idea at noon.

3. (A) She is not sure how to get information.
   (B) She does not know if the college has a number.

   (C) She suggests asking information for the college number.
   (D) She does not know if the college is in Texas.

4. (A) He does not like either one.
   (B) He does not want to go to either one.
   (C) The play and the movie are about the same subject.
   (D) It makes no difference to him which they go to.

GO ON TO THE NEXT PAGE

5. (A) Study with his friends at the library.
   (B) Stay at school.
   (C) Study alone in the library.
   (D) Go home and study.

6. (A) Peter.
   (B) Nancy.
   (C) John.
   (D) An office worker.

7. (A) Susan has been in this country for less than a year.
   (B) Susan has been in this country for more than a year.
   (C) Susan has been in this country for a very long time.
   (D) Susan will be in this country for another year at least.

8. (A) He thinks the sound is good in the front row.
   (B) He agrees that the sound is good near the front.
   (C) He thinks it is a good idea to sit in the front row.
   (D) He will hear better in the front row.

9. (A) It's too loud.
   (B) It's a good song.
   (C) The volume is too low.
   (D) The song is too slow.

10. (A) It's difficult for her to say American first names.
    (B) American customs are difficult.
    (C) American professors use first names.
    (D) Using first names in America worries her.

11. (A) John would never go along to the meeting.
    (B) Having John along at the meeting is a good idea.
    (C) Bringing John along at the meeting is a good idea.
    (D) It would be terrible to bring John to the meeting.

12. (A) The lecture was not very good.

(B) This lecture was better than the last one he heard.
(C) He feels better after he heard the lecture.
(D) He was able to hear the lecture better than last time.

13. (A) She wants to go to the presentation, but not alone.
    (B) She doesn't really want to go to the presentation.
    (C) She'll go to the presentation if it's in the auditorium.
    (D) She has to attend tonight's presentation because it's the only one.

14. (A) Jim promised to be back by Monday.
    (B) Jim will take her to the airport after work on Monday.
    (C) Jim promised to take her, but it's not on his way to work.
    (D) Jim will take her before he goes to work on Monday.

15. (A) He finished his novel and started his term paper.
    (B) He finished his term paper and started a novel.
    (C) He has just finished his term paper.
    (D) He hasn't finished his term paper.

16. (A) Painting a house.
    (B) Planting a garden.
    (C) Taking an art class.
    (D) Refinishing furniture.

17. (A) She missed seeing the castles and museums on her vacation.
    (B) She went without a vacation just to see the castles and museums.
    (C) She had a good vacation in general, but didn't like the castles and museums.
    (D) She would rather not have taken a vacation than gone to all those castles and museums.

GO ON TO THE NEXT PAGE

18. (A) He'll arrive at the party after a while.
    (B) He's showing off by not arriving at the party on time.
    (C) He had a show to go to instead of the party.
    (D) He was too worried to go to the party.

19. (A) He's jumped so many times that now he has a limp.
    (B) He hurt himself the last time he jumped.
    (C) He's afraid to jump, so he's pretending to be limping.
    (D) He's wanted to ski jump many times, but can't because he limps.

20. (A) He didn't know how to make potato salad.
    (B) He didn't think the weather was good enough for a picnic.
    (C) He didn't like to bring things to a picnic.
    (D) He wasn't going to go to the picnic.

21. (A) She doesn't like to read books.
    (B) She likes to be outdoors when it rains.
    (C) It's a long time since she had plans for the weekend.
    (D) The rain spoiled her weekend plans.

22. (A) To park the man's car for him.
    (B) To write up a prescription for a new walking device.
    (C) To make access to places easier for the man.
    (D) To give the man driving lessons.

23. (A) They were very proud of him.
    (B) They ran up the stairs to the attic.
    (C) They were upset.
    (D) They acted as calmly as he'd expected.

24. (A) She could have talked to David's professor for him.
    (B) She could have helped David find his resources.
    (C) She could have given David a lecture.
    (D) David could have done the woman's research for her.

25. (A) That Jeremy was going to break something in biology lab.
    (B) That Jeremy was hoping biology lab would be canceled.
    (C) That Jeremy might faint in biology lab.
    (D) That Jeremy was thinking of quitting biology.

26. (A) Dentist.
    (B) Construction worker.
    (C) Plastic surgeon.
    (D) Sculptor.

27. (A) The man should invite her cousin to the dance.
    (B) The man should ask her cousin how she's feeling.
    (C) The man should dance with the woman and her cousin.
    (D) The man should see her cousin on Thursday.

28. (A) Take notes for her in English literature class.
    (B) Take care of her after her run.
    (C) Put away her lab equipment for her.
    (D) Teach the English literature class for her.

29. (A) He caught a bad cold.
    (B) He lost his courage.
    (C) He was unkind.
    (D) He spoke very plainly.

30. (A) Sean and Patsy don't like each other.
    (B) Sean doesn't know what the weather is like outside.
    (C) Patsy didn't know that Sean dislikes the botanical gardens.
    (D) Sean and Patsy can't agree on how to spend the day.

GO ON TO THE NEXT PAGE

Part B

<u>Directions</u>: In this part, you will hear longer conversations. After each conversation, you will be asked several questions. You will hear the conversations and the questions about them only one time. They will not be repeated. Therefore, you must listen carefully to understand what each speaker says.

After you hear a question, read the four possible answers in your test book and choose which <u>one</u> is the best answer to the question you heard. Then, on your answer sheet, find the number of the question and fill in the space that corresponds to the letter of the answer you have chosen.

Remember, you should not take notes or write on your test paper.

31. (A) Japanese management.
    (B) Comparative cultures.
    (C) Two students' research paper topics.
    (D) How to research sources.

32. (A) They are both taking World Economics.
    (B) They are going to the same graduate school.
    (C) They are going to Japan.
    (D) They're both writing papers on a similar topic.

33. (A) Have a snack.
    (B) Go to the library.
    (C) Exchange information about sources.
    (D) Look for sources at the snack bar.

34. (A) A department store.
    (B) A stock exchange.
    (C) A bank.
    (D) A university.

35. (A) A bank teller and a patron.
    (B) An accounts manager and a customer.
    (C) A sales clerk and a shopper.
    (D) A stock broker and a client.

36. (A) Charge.
    (B) Checking.
    (C) Stocks and bonds.
    (D) Savings.

37. (A) She thinks it's unreasonable.
    (B) She thinks it should have been implemented sooner.
    (C) She thinks it makes good sense.
    (D) She thinks it's good business.

38. (A) Take her business someplace else.
    (B) Open an account.
    (C) Talk to the manager.
    (D) Charge her purchases.

GO ON TO THE NEXT PAGE

Part C

<u>Directions</u>: In this part, you will hear various talks. After each talk, you will be asked several questions. The talks and questions will not be repeated. They will not be written out for you. Therefore, you must listen carefully to understand what the speaker says.

After you hear a question, read the four possible answers in your test book and choose which one is the best answer to the question you heard. Then, on your answer sheet, find the number of the question and fill in the space that corresponds to the letter of the answer you have chosen.

Listen to this sample talk.

You will hear: **The National Health Research Center, perhaps more than any other organization, will directly affect the lives of millions of Americans every day. The Health Research Center volunteers will work all over the United States to provide information on diet and lifestyles. The bulk of the foundation's time will be spent conducting seminars and distributing pamphlets on how to prevent major illness and increase longevity. A free long-distance 800 number is available for anyone with health-related questions.**

Now listen to the following question.

What is the speaker's purpose?

You will read: (A) To get you to join the foundation.
(B) To inform you of the existence of the Health Research Center.
(C) To persuade you to give a donation to the foundation.
(D) To ask you to distribute pamphlets for the foundation.

The best answer to the question, "What is the speaker's purpose?" is *To inform you of the existence of the Health Research Center.* Therefore, you should choose answer (B).

<u>Sample Answer</u>
Ⓐ ● Ⓒ Ⓓ

Now listen to the next example.

Why would you use the center's 800 number?

You will read: (A) To volunteer to distribute pamphlets.
(B) To make a contribution to the Health Research Center.
(C) To obtain a schedule of seminars.
(D) To ask questions regarding good health.

The best answer to the question, "Why would you use the center's 800 number?" is *To ask questions regarding good health.* Therefore, you should choose answer (D).

<u>Sample Answer</u>
Ⓐ Ⓑ Ⓒ ●

39. (A) The importance of giving the correct location in an emergency.
(B) The necessity of owning a fire or security alarm.
(C) The advantages of owning the alarm radio transmitter.
(D) The cost savings of buying during the 25% sale.

GO ON TO THE NEXT PAGE

40. (A) To inform the audience on how to contact emergency services.
    (B) To persuade the audience to purchase a radio transmitter.
    (C) To tell the audience that their family's safety is important.
    (D) To describe the best procedures in an emergency.

41. (A) Emergency telephone operator.
    (B) Police officer.
    (C) Radio repair person.
    (D) Sales representative.

42. (A) Who is contacted in an emergency.
    (B) Where the police and fire departments are located.
    (C) How quickly emergency services are contacted.
    (D) What kind of emergency is taking place.

43. (A) Transmits the location of the emergency.
    (B) Makes the emergency call.
    (C) Gives the exact location of the nearest emergency service.
    (D) Protects a family in an emergency.

44. (A) A representative from the admissions office.
    (B) A representative from the registrar's office.
    (C) The international student advisor.
    (D) The president of the college.

45. (A) The speaker.
    (B) The international student advisor.
    (C) An international student.
    (D) A representative from the registrar's office.

46. (A) Someone from the admissions office will come next week to answer questions.
    (B) The international student advisor will answer questions.
    (C) Someone from the registrar's office will answer questions.
    (D) There will be a question and answer session next week.

47. (A) Every month.
    (B) Every week.
    (C) Every semester.
    (D) Every year.

48. (A) How beetles walk.
    (B) Insect behavior.
    (C) How insects walk on ceilings.
    (D) How insects use three legs to move forward.

49. (A) In a classroom.
    (B) At an art exhibit.
    (C) In a university library.
    (D) At the restaurant.

50. (A) By supporting themselves on three legs.
    (B) By using claws and pulvilli.
    (C) By means of tiny projections on their claws.
    (D) By means of cushions on their legs.

THIS IS THE END OF THE LISTENING COMPREHENSION SECTION OF THE TEST

THE NEXT PART OF THE TEST IS SECTION 2.
TURN TO THE DIRECTIONS FOR SECTION 2 IN YOUR TEST BOOK.
READ THEM AND BEGIN WORK.
DO NOT READ OR WORK ON ANY OTHER SECTION OF THE TEST.

SECTION 2
STRUCTURE AND WRITTEN EXPRESSION

Time – 25 minutes

This section is designed to measure your ability to recognize language that is appropriate for standard written English. There are two types of questions in this section, with special directions for each type.

<u>Directions:</u> Questions 1-15 are incomplete sentences. Beneath each sentence you will see four words or phrases, marked (A), (B), (C), and (D). Choose the <u>one</u> word or phrase that best completes the sentence. Then, on your answer sheet, find the number of the question and fill in the space that corresponds to the letter of the answer you have chosen. Fill in the space so that the letter inside the oval cannot be seen.

Example I

    Sound comes in waves, and the
    higher the frequency, ...
    (A) higher is the pitch.
    (B) the pitch is higher.
    (C) the higher the pitch.
    (D) pitch is the higher.

The sentence should read, "Sound comes in waves, and the higher the frequency, the higher the pitch." Therefore, you should choose answer (C).

Example II

    Fire safety in family houses, ...
    most fire deaths occur, is difficult
    to achieve.
    (A) where
    (B) why
    (C) how
    (D) when

<u>Sample Answer</u>
Ⓐ Ⓑ ● Ⓓ

The sentence should read, "Fire safety in family houses, where most fire deaths occur, is difficult to achieve." Therefore, you should choose answer (A).

After you read the directions, begin work on the questions.

<u>Sample Answer</u>
● Ⓑ Ⓒ Ⓓ

1. . . . . . is a poison when ingested above trace amounts.
   (A) It is lead
   (B) Lead
   (C) The lead
   (D) That lead

2. . . . . . its outstanding hardness, the less valuable forms of the diamond are used by industry in the manufacture of cutting tools.
   (A) Because of
   (B) Beyond
   (C) Such as
   (D) In spite of

3. Most snakes eat animals . . . . . in proportion to their own size.
   (A) they are
   (B) large
   (C) that are large
   (D) are large

4. Noise is known . . . . . constriction of the smaller arteries.
   (A) causing
   (B) cause
   (C) causes
   (D) to cause

5. Bees find their way to the nectar in a flower . . . . . differences in the humidity of the air.
   (A) by senses
   (B) by sensing
   (C) sense
   (D) sensed

6. . . . . . the film used for Cinemascope is the same as for conventional pictures, the image produced has twice the normal width.
   (A) Yet
   (B) However
   (C) Although
   (D) As

7. After World War I, Hollywood emerged . . . . . the movie capital of the world.
   (A) as
   (B) like
   (C) such as
   (D) in

8. Christopher Sholes, a printer, developed a typewriter . . . . . first sold by the Remington Arms Company in 1875.
   (A) it was
   (B) that it was
   (C) that has been
   (D) that was

9. Calcium is not only found in dairy produce . . . . . found in many dark green vegetables.
   (A) that is also
   (B) and is also
   (C) but is also
   (D) also it is

10. In the 1920s, a new plastic called cellophane . . . . . as an alternative to wrapping paper.
    (A) it developed
    (B) was developed
    (C) that was developed
    (D) developed

11. Georgia O'Keefe . . . . . of skyscrapers in her early paintings and later turned to Southwestern themes.
    (A) celebrated urban landscapes
    (B) who celebrated urban landscapes
    (C) was urban landscapes celebrating
    (D) whose urban landscapes were celebrated

GO ON TO THE NEXT PAGE

12. Greenhouse gases, like carbon dioxide, accumulate in the atmosphere and . . . . . from escaping from the planet.
    (A) to prevent the sun's heat
    (B) the sun's heat prevent
    (C) prevent the sun's heat
    (D) the sun's heat prevents

13. The basic source of calories is glucose, ... produced by plants.
    (A) a sugar
    (B) sugar
    (C) is a sugar
    (D) which it is a sugar

14. There is no water on the moon, nor . . . . . an atmosphere around it.
    (A) there is
    (B) it is
    (C) there is not
    (D) is there

15. In the 1800s, industrial expansion was greatest in the North, ... the development of the railroad systems.
    (A) and as
    (B) as was
    (C) also
    (D) was also

Directions: Questions 16-40 each sentence had four underlined words or phrases. The four underlined parts of the sentence are marked (A), (B), (C), and (D). Identify the one underlined word or phrase that must be changed in order for the sentence to be correct. Then, on your answer sheet, find the number of the question and fill in the space that corresponds to the letter of the answer you have chosen.

Example I

After Newton has observed an apple fall
            A   B
to the ground, he formulated the law of
                                 C
gravity.
   D

The underlined words has observed would not be acceptable in carefully written English. The past perfect form of the verb should be used to express the first of two completed actions in the past. Therefore, the sentence should read, "After Newton had observed an apple fall to the ground, he formulated the law of gravity." To answer the question correctly, you should choose (A).

Sample Answer
● Ⓑ Ⓒ Ⓓ

GO ON TO THE NEXT PAGE ➡

Example II

In 1740, John Newbery was <u>the</u>
                                    A
first publisher <u>to produce</u>
                       B
books <u>which</u> children really
              C
wanted <u>read</u>.
             D

The underlined word <u>read</u> would not be accepted in carefully written English; the infinitive form to read should be used because the verb wanted takes an infinitive with "to." Therefore, the sentence should read, "In 1740, John Newbery was the first publisher to produce books which children really wanted to read." To answer the question correctly, you should choose (D).

<u>Sample Answer</u>
Ⓐ Ⓑ Ⓒ ●

After you read the directions, begin work on the questions.

16. Thermometric study is <u>essential</u> to human welfare <u>because</u> all people on earth <u>are effected</u>
                                    A   B   C
by temperature, <u>natural</u> or man-made.
                           D

17. One of the biggest <u>changes</u> in the American economy during the past three decades <u>has been</u>
                               A   B
<u>a</u> influx <u>of</u> women into the wage-earning work force.
  C   D

18. Grant Wood <u>painted</u> scenes of rural America, including his <u>memorable</u> portrait of <u>a</u>
                         A   B   C
<u>farm somber</u> couple, *American Gothic*, in 1930.
       D

19. <u>African elephant</u>, found today in Africa, is <u>distinguishable</u> by <u>its</u> large and <u>constantly</u> moving
          A   B   C   D
ears, which cool the blood that circulates through them.

20. Each star <u>has</u> <u>a</u> predominant color, which <u>depend</u> <u>on</u> its surface temperature.
                    A B   C   D

21. The distribution of copper, like <u>that</u> of gold, <u>does not</u> appear to be <u>related</u> to any <u>particularly</u>
                                                A   B   C   D
type of rock.

GO ON TO THE NEXT PAGE ➤

22. <u>No matter</u> what language <u>he is</u> learning, children all seem <u>to follow</u> the same order <u>in</u> the
    A   B   C   D

    acquisition of sounds.

23. Most rodents <u>are</u> nocturnal animals, so <u>therefore</u> their most developed senses are <u>hearing</u>,
               A   B   C

    smell, and <u>touching</u>.
             D

24. Tornadoes <u>they are</u> the smallest, yet the <u>most violent</u> of the major <u>storm</u> <u>types</u>.
          A   B   C   D

25. Bone cells <u>are nourished</u> by a fluid called plasma, <u>derived</u> from <u>the</u> blood, but containing
              A   B   C

    neither the red <u>or</u> the white corpuscles.
                  D

26. Active faults are dangerous areas for settlement, <u>unless</u> buildings <u>constructed</u> <u>especially</u> to
                                      A   B   C

    avoid <u>earthquake</u> damage.
         D

27. Warm, <u>shallow</u>, clear <u>sea water</u>, free from silts or clays, <u>are required</u> <u>for</u> all coral-reef
           A   B   C   D

    development.

28. The most important cause of <u>tides</u> is the <u>gravitation</u> <u>attraction</u> of <u>the</u> moon.
                           A   B   C   D

29. Normal blood pressure <u>usually varies</u> from moment to moment, <u>depending of</u> your <u>degree of</u>
                            A   B   C

    physical and mental <u>relaxation</u>.
                  D

30. <u>Theol</u>, the <u>essential</u> oil in the tea leaf, gives the <u>flavor</u> and <u>aromatic</u>.
    A   B   C   D

31. The destructive <u>effects of</u> air pollution <u>on</u> plants can be long <u>lasting</u> <u>as well</u> widespread.
                  A   B   C   D

32. Many marine birds and reptiles are <u>equipped with</u> special glands that are <u>exclusive</u> used <u>for</u>
                               A   B   C

    <u>salt removal</u>.
       D

33. Saturated fat <u>is almost</u> always found in the same <u>foods</u> that contain high levels of cholesterol,
             A   B

    except shellfish, <u>which have</u> very <u>few fat</u>.
                C   D

GO ON TO THE NEXT PAGE ➤

34. The early American press <u>has consisted</u> <u>almost entirely</u> <u>of</u> what we <u>would call</u> editorials.
                          A   B   C   D

35. In a <u>typical</u> giant corporation, directors and managers own <u>least</u> five percent <u>of the</u> common
           A   B   C
<u>stock</u>.
  D

36. The bald eagle <u>was chosen</u> <u>as</u> <u>the emblem</u> of the United States because it is <u>a native</u> to North
                      A   B   C   D
America.

37. In the 1890s, the electric trolley could go twice as <u>fast</u> and <u>carry</u> three times <u>as much</u> passengers
                                                   A   B   C
<u>as</u> the horse-drawn trolley.
D

38. Every sound <u>what</u> occurs <u>in</u> human languages can be represented <u>by means</u> <u>of</u> the phonetic
                   A   B   C   D
alphabet.

39. The most important <u>method saving</u> by individuals in recent years <u>has been</u> real estate investment,
                             A   B
particularly <u>in</u> <u>private</u> dwellings.
           C   D

40. Telephoto, <u>a</u> process for <u>sending</u> pictures by wire, <u>has been invented</u> during the 1920s, and the
           A   B   C
first transcontinental telephoto <u>was</u> sent in 1925.
                              D

3 • 3 • 3 • 3 • 3 • 3 • 3

SECTION 3
READING COMPREHENSION

Time – 55 minutes

This section is designed to measure your comprehension of standard written English.

Directions: In this section, you will read several passages. Each is followed by a number of questions about it. For questions 1-50, you are to choose the one best answer, (A), (B), (C), or (D), to each question. Then on your answer sheet, find the number of the question and fill in the space that corresponds to the letter of the answer you have chosen.

Answer all questions about the information in a passage on the basis of what is stated or implied in that passage.

Read the following passage:

The Mediterranean fruit fly is one of the world's most destructive insect pests. It attacks more than 250 kinds of fruits, nuts, and vegetables. If the pest made its way into fruit and vegetable-growing parts of the United States, supplies of produce would go down and prices would go up. It would devastate commercial agriculture and could cost consumers an estimated additional $820 million per year.

5

Example I

What is the main idea of the passage?
(A) Farmers need to produce more as a result of the Medfly.
(B) Commercial agriculture is very expensive in the United States.
(C) People should be aware of the danger of the Medfly.
(D) Many fruits and vegetables are infested by the Medfly in the United States.

The main idea of the passage is to warn people about the danger of the Medfly. Therefore, you should choose answer (C).

Sample Answer
Ⓐ Ⓑ ● Ⓓ

Example II

In line 3, the word "It" refers to
(A) commercial agriculture.
(B) supplies of produce.
(C) The Mediterranean fruit fly.
(D) $820 million.

The word "It" refers to "if the pest made its way," the pest is the Medfly, so you should choose answer (C).

Sample Answer
Ⓐ Ⓑ ● Ⓓ

Now begin work on the questions.

GO ON TO THE NEXT PAGE →

Questions 1 -10

In a quiet rural setting 30 miles northwest of Boston, there, atop a hill overlooking an apple orchard and the remnants of a pumpkin patch, sits a dish-shaped antenna, 80ft across, facing skyward, and attuned to the murmurings of the cosmos.

5 That antenna is a Harvard-Smithsonian radio telescope, the ear of the newly dedicated project BETA (Billion-channel Extra-Terrestrial Assay), the latest and most ambitious effort yet in the Search for Extra-Terrestrial Intelligence (SETI). The search has been doggedly conducted over four decades by small bands of devoted scientists around the world. It is a quest not only for life beyond the Earth, but for life intelligent and capable enough to transmit meaningful radio signals across vast stretches of empty space.

10 Inside BETA's one-story control room, a work station displays patterns of green and red spikes. Lights blink on a bank of small computers, and needles flutter on glowing dials. From a stereo amplifier comes a static-filled hiss, the audio version of radio waves piped directly from the antenna above. But, except for graduate student Darren Leigh, hard at work debugging a BETA computer program, the room is empty. BETA is, with good reason, an almost entirely automated

15 experiment. Otherwise, as BETA Director and Harvard physicist Paul Horowitz puts it, "What do you do when something comes in the middle of the night and there's no one here to listen?"

Horowitz is dedicated to SETI, convinced that life is out there for the finding. "I have no doubts," he says. "Intelligent life in the universe? Guaranteed. Intelligent life in our galaxy? So overwhelmingly likely that I'd give you almost any odds you'd like." Still, Horowitz is realistic.

20 "The hard part is the last step, which is intelligent beings in the galaxy transmitting radio waves to us at a wavelength that we're expecting and at a power level such that we can detect them." "That," he concedes, "is a lot of ifs."

1. What does the passage mainly discuss?
   (A) The Harvard-Smith radio telescope
   (B) Projects within SETI
   (C) The control room at BETA
   (D) Horowitz's ideas about SETI

2. The word "murmurings" in line 3 is closest in meaning to
   (A) patterns.
   (B) sounds.
   (C) lights.
   (D) flashes.

3. It can be inferred from the passage that the telescope is in a rural area because
   (A) it is too large to site in a city.
   (B) the air in cities is too polluted.
   (C) there is less interference from noise.
   (D) it is easier for scientist to work there.

4. The word "It" in line 7 refers to
   (A) search.
   (B) antenna.
   (C) effort.
   (D) life.

5. The "hiss" in line 12 is caused by the
   (A) green and red spikes.
   (B) stereo amplifier.
   (C) radio waves.
   (D) antenna.

6. What is Horowitz implying in his question (lines 15-16)?
   (A) There should always be someone in BETA's control room.
   (B) Although the system is automated, someone is needed to interpret the signals.
   (C) It is not necessary for someone to be present at BETA all the time.
   (D) As the system is automated, there is no necessity for anyone to be involved at all.

GO ON TO THE NEXT PAGE

7. The word "Guaranteed" in line 18 could best be replaced by
   (A) definite.
   (B) tested.
   (C) apparent.
   (D) certified.

8. According to the passage, one of the problems for scientists if they receive radio signals is they may
   (A) include strange information.
   (B) be transmitted at a low level.
   (C) come from an unknown galaxy.
   (D) be on a foreign wavelength.

9. What does Horowitz mean when he says, "I'd give you any odds you'd like."?
   (A) He wants you to believe in SETI.
   (B) He's prepared to offer you money.
   (C) He's sure he is correct.
   (D) He thinks he'd like to change your mind.

10. According to the passage, the possibility that the radio telescope will receive SETI signals is
   (A) certain.
   (B) doubtful.
   (C) likely.
   (D) negligible.

Questions 11 - 20

For more than 25 years, the video artist, Bill Viola, has consistently used the most contemporary electronic technologies to create deceptively simple videotapes and video-and-sound installations. They pursue an ancient theme: the revelation of the layers of human consciousness. Although based on realistic images, his projects go beyond representation to challenge the viewer's
5 preconceived expectations. His work probes many levels of experience. As he has said, "The real investigation is of life and being itself. The medium is just the tool in this investigation."

He gives painstaking attention to his subjects, both natural and man-made, so the results invariably have a beauty, intensity, and depth of spirit. He handles his recorded images in a straightforward manner. The primary special effects he employs involve slowing down, reversing,
10 or speeding up time. This directness extends to his editing, which is as concise as it is precise. Nothing is extraneous and very little left to chance. Because he is exceptionally skillful with, and knowledgeable about, video equipment, he is free to be creative during production. He works alone, without needing the assistance of a technician, so each project remains an expression of his personal vision.
15 His primary subject is the physical and mental worlds, the connections between inner and outer realms. He is concerned with exploring the interaction of his images with the viewer's memory as well as with the subconscious and dreams. He thinks of memory as a filter, an editing process which is going on all the time. In the memory, images are created and transformed and it is as much about the future as it is about the past. Viola in interested in how thought is a function of
20 time.

GO ON TO THE NEXT PAGE

11. What does the passage mainly discuss?
    (A) Bill Viola's technological skill
    (B) The aims of Bill Viola's work
    (C) Bill Viola's working methods
    (D) The video installations of Bill Viola

12. Which of the following is NOT mentioned as a theme of Bill Viola's work?
    (A) Consciousness
    (B) Dreams
    (C) Beauty
    (D) Memory

13. The word "revelation" in line 3 is closest in meaning to
    (A) outcome.
    (B) explanation.
    (C) appearance.
    (D) disclosure.

14. According to the passage, how does Bill Viola achieve special effects?
    (A) By using filters
    (B) By skilled editing
    (C) By manipulating videotape
    (D) By installing videos

15. What does Bill Viola mean by the statement, "The medium is just the tool in this investigation."?
    (A) The videotape installations are only a means to explore Bill Viola's ideas.
    (B) Bill Viola's ideas can only be investigated through using advanced electronic equipment.
    (C) Without electronic technology it is impossible for Bill Viola to have ideas to explore.
    (D) Using videotape gives Bill Viola themes to investigate.

16. It can be inferred from the passage that Bill Viola's prime purpose for producing his work is to
    (A) trigger memory through visuals.
    (B) give people new experiences.
    (C) explore the natural world.
    (D) produce something of beauty.

17. The phrase "very little left to chance" (line 11) could be replaced by
    (A) practically nothing depends on luck.
    (B) a few things depend on good fortune.
    (C) nearly everything is carefully planned.
    (D) occasionally a chance is taken on editing.

18. The word "it" in line 18 refers to
    (A) created.
    (B) past.
    (C) transformed.
    (D) memory.

19. From the passage, it can be inferred that Bill Viola likes working alone because he
    (A) needs freedom in the studio.
    (B) creates while working.
    (C) doesn't trust technicians.
    (D) doesn't like interruptions.

20. Where in the passage does the author suggest that Bill Viola can lengthen time?
    (A) Lines 1 - 2
    (B) Lines 8 - 10
    (C) Lines 17 - 18
    (D) Lines 19 - 20

GO ON TO THE NEXT PAGE

Questions 21 - 30

The aspect of language use that is most worth changing is the clarity and style of written prose. Expository writing requires language to express far more complex trains of thought than it was biologically designed to do. Inconsistencies caused by limitations of short-term memory and planning, unnoticed in conversation, are not as tolerable when preserved on a page that is to be
5 perused more leisurely. Also, unlike a conversational partner, a reader will rarely share enough background assumptions to interpolate all the missing premises that make language comprehensible. Overcoming one's natural egocentrism and trying to anticipate the knowledge state of a reader at every stage of the exposition is one of the most important tasks in writing well. All this makes writing a difficult craft that must be mastered through practice, instruction,
10 feedback, and – probably most important – intensive exposure to good examples. There are excellent manuals of composition that discuss these and other skills with great wisdom. What is most relevant is how removed their practical advice is from the trivia of split infinitives and slang. For example, a banal but universally acknowledged key to good writing is to revise extensively. Good writers go through anywhere from two to twenty drafts before releasing a
15 paper. Anyone who does not appreciate this necessity is going to be a bad writer. If clear writing is wanted, then this is the course that must be followed.

21. What is the main topic of the passage?
    (A) The importance of repeated drafting in writing
    (B) The difficulties involved in producing good writing
    (C) The problems of conveying meaning to readers
    (D) The importance of reading good writing

22. The phrase "trains of thought" is closest in meaning to
    (A) ways of thinking.
    (B) connected ideas.
    (C) continuous concepts.
    (D) logical thinking.

23. Why does the author mention "short-term memory" in line 3?
    (A) To suggest that memories are not always accurate
    (B) To show the problems of writing down memories
    (C) To indicate the necessity for long-term memory
    (D) To explain short-term memory is inadequate for complex writing

24. According to the passage, readers sometimes have difficulty understanding texts because
    (A) they have no knowledge of the subject matter.
    (B) there is no opportunity for them to check their assumptions.
    (C) they assume that the texts are too difficult.
    (D) some ideas are unconnected in the texts.

25. It can be inferred from the passage that good writers
    (A) are self-centered.
    (B) consider their readers.
    (C) convey knowledge precisely.
    (D) explain every point.

26. The word "exposure" in line 10 could best be replaced by
    (A) access.
    (B) detection.
    (C) approach.
    (D) pursuit.

GO ON TO THE NEXT PAGE

27. The author suggests that the best books about writing
    (A) contain explanations about grammar.
    (B) explain colloquial expressions.
    (C) include examples of good writing.
    (D) concentrate on writing skills.

28. The word "banal" in line 13 is closest in meaning to
    (A) weak.
    (B) poor.
    (C) common.
    (D) modest.

29. The word "this" in line 16 refers to
    (A) extensive drafting.
    (B) practical advice.
    (C) acknowledged key.
    (D) intensive exposure.

30. The passage supports which of the following conclusions
    (A) Conveying meaning in writing is easier than in conversation.
    (B) Writing can be learned from a good manual.
    (C) There is no substitute for revision in good writing.
    (D) Writing is a biological process with its own styles.

Questions 31 - 40

The principle of use and disuse states that those parts of organisms' bodies that are used grow larger. Those parts that are not tend to whither away. It is an observed fact that when you excercise particular muscles, they grow. Those that are never used diminish. By examining a man's body, we can tell which muscles he uses and which he does not. We may even be able to guess his
5 profession or his recreation. Enthusiasts of the "body-building" cult make use of the principle of use and disuse to "build" their bodies, almost like a piece of sculpture, into whatever unnatural shape is demanded by fashion in this peculiar minority culture. Muscles are not the only parts of the body that respond to use in this kind of way. Walk barefoot and you acquire harder skin on your soles. It is easy to tell a farmer from a bank teller by looking at their hands alone. The
10 farmer's hands are horny, hardened by long exposure to rough work. The teller's hands are relatively soft.
    The principle of use and disuse enables animals to become better at the job of surviving in their world, progressively better during their lifetime as a result of living in that world. Humans, through direct exposure to sunlight, or lack of it, develop a skin color which equips them better to
15 survive in the particular local conditions. Too much sunlight is dangerous. Enthusiastic sunbathers with very fair skins are susceptible to skin cancer. Too little sunlight, on the other hand, leads to vitamin-D deficiency and rickets. The brown pigment melanin which is synthesized under the influence of sunlight, makes a screen to protect the underlying tissues from the harmful effects of further sunlight. If a suntanned person moves to a less sunny climate, the
20 melanin disappears, and the body is able to benefit from what little sun there is. This can be represented as an instance of the principle of use and disuse: skin goes brown when it is "used," and fades to white when it is not.

GO ON TO THE NEXT PAGE

31. What does the passage mainly discuss?
    (A) How the principles of use and disuse change people's concepts of themselves
    (B) The way in which people change themselves to conform to fashion
    (C) The changes that occur according to the principle of use and disuse
    (D) The effects of the sun on the principle of use and disuse

32. The phrase "whither away" in line 2 is closest in meaning to
    (A) split.
    (B) rot.
    (C) perish.
    (D) shrink.

33. The word "Those" in line 3 refers to
    (A) organisms.
    (B) bodies.
    (C) parts.
    (D) muscles.

34. According to the passage, men who body build
    (A) appear like sculptures.
    (B) change their appearance.
    (C) belong to strange cults.
    (D) are very fashionable.

35. From the passage, it can be inferred that the author views body building
    (A) with enthusiasm.
    (B) as an artistic form.
    (C) with scientific interest.
    (D) of doubtful benefit.

36. The word "horny" in line 10 is closest in meaning to
    (A) firm.
    (B) strong.
    (C) tough.
    (D) dense.

37. It can be inferred from the passage that the principle of use and disuse enables organisms to
    (A) change their existence.
    (B) automatically benefit.
    (C) survive in any conditions.
    (D) improve their lifetime.

38. The author suggests that melanin
    (A) is necessary for the production of vitamin-D.
    (B) is beneficial in sunless climates.
    (C) helps protect fair-skinned people.
    (D) is a synthetic product.

39. In the second paragraph, the author mentions suntanning as an example of
    (A) humans improving their local condition.
    (B) humans surviving in adverse conditions.
    (C) humans using the principle of use and disuse.
    (D) humans running the risk of skin cancer.

40. The word "susceptible" could best be replaced by
    (A) condemned.
    (B) vulnerable.
    (C) allergic.
    (D) suggestible.

GO ON TO THE NEXT PAGE

Questions 41 - 50

The playwright and director Robert Wilson's theatrical technique represents a significant departure from customary forms of dramatic story-telling. Events rarely occur in sequence and follow no discernible casual pattern. Like a dream or hallucination, the action of a Wilson "play" takes shape, dissolves, overlaps, fragments, and reforms. Two or three "stories" may be told
5 simultaneously, using characters drawn from different historical epochs, from different geographical locations. Each scene functions as a "construction in time and space," or, more accurately, as painting in motion, designed to break down normal spatial and temporal ideas for the sake of new perceptual experiences.

   In Wilson, why his characters move may be less significant than how they move. One intently
10 watches the move itself, with sufficient time to meditate on its form rather than its purpose. He asks his audience to absorb his images almost subliminally, not to insist on immediate understanding of his work. "If you see a Japanese garden" he says, "you can be attracted to its beauty without understanding why all the elements are placed where they are. Similarly, in the theater, one doesn't make all of the connections during the course of the play. One begins to put
15 them together afterwards."

   There is a precedent for Wilson's theater. It is found in oriental theater, particularly in the Japanese drama of Noh, elements of which appear in Wilson's plays. Emphasizing symbol, image, metaphor, dream, and icon, he leaves his audience free to daydream or hallucinate, to relax (even to sleep), without forcing them into rational conclusions. "We try not to interfere with the
20 interpretation," he says. "We merely present the ideas."

41. The passage primarily discusses
    (A) painting.
    (B) history.
    (C) drama.
    (D) geography.

42. The word "discernible" in line 3 is closest in meaning to
    (A) visualize.
    (B) detractable.
    (C) recognizable.
    (D) impressionable.

43. According to the passage, Robert Wilson designs his plays to
    (A) provide fresh insights.
    (B) awaken critical senses.
    (C) encourage historical research.
    (D) display dramatic principles.

44. Robert Wilson says the way his characters move is more important than why, because they represent
    (A) paintings.
    (B) forms.
    (C) reasons.
    (D) functions.

45. The word "meditate" in line 10 could best be replaced by
    (A) concentrate.
    (B) imagine.
    (C) cogitate.
    (D) contemplate.

46. It can be inferred from the passage that Robert Wilson is more interested in the audience's
    (A) irrational feelings.
    (B) subconscious absorption.
    (C) perceptual ideas.
    (D) mental processes.

GO ON TO THE NEXT PAGE

47. All of the following elements are present in a Robert Wilson play EXCEPT
    (A) causes and effects.
    (B) subliminal ideas.
    (C) symbolic actions.
    (D) fragmented images.

48. The word "it" in line 16 refers to
    (A) play.
    (B) precedent.
    (C) drama.
    (D) theater.

49. The word "rational" in line 19 is closest in meaning to
    (A) philosophical.
    (B) intellectual.
    (C) logical.
    (D) conceptual.

50. The passage supports which of the following conclusions?
    (A) R.W.'s drama is independent of traditional forms.
    (B) R.W.'s plays are based on ritualistic ideas.
    (C) R.W.'s "stories" are constructed around formal concepts.
    (D) R.W.'s constructs are founded on oriental philosophy.

THIS IS THE END OF SECTION 3

IF YOU FINISH BEFORE TIME IS CALLED, CHECK YOUR WORK ON SECTION 3 ONLY.
DO NOT READ OR WORK ON ANY OTHER SECTION OF THE TEST.

TEST OF WRITTEN ENGLISH ESSAY QUESTION

Time – 30 minutes

SOME PEOPLE SAY THAT LEARNING A FOREIGN LANGUAGE IS EXTREMELY
IMPORTANT. OTHERS SAY THAT STUDYING A SCIENCE IS MORE USEFUL.

Discuss these positions, using specific examples of each.
Say which one you agree with and explain why.

TAPESCRIPTS
Practice Test 1

LISTENING COMPREHENSION

In this section of the test, you will have an opportunity to demonstrate your ability to understand conversations and talks in English. In this section, there are answers to all the questions based on the information heard.

Part A

Directions: In Part A, you will hear short conversations between two people. At the end of each conversation, you will hear a question about the conversation. The conversation and question will not be repeated. Therefore, you must listen carefully to understand what each speaker says. After you hear a question, read the four possible answers in your test book and choose the best answer to the question you heard. Then, on your answer sheet, find the number of the question and fill in the space that corresponds to the letter of the answer you have chosen.

Listen to an example on the recording:

Man:	**What seems to be the problem, ma'am?**
Woman:	**Well, the light switch is broken and a plug needs repairing.**
Question:	**What kind of work does the man probably do?**

In your book you will read:
(A) He's a carpenter.
(B) He's a plumber.
(C) He's an electrician.
(D) He's an engineer.

From the conversation, you learn that the light switch is broken and a plug needs repairing. The best answer to the question, "What kind of work does the man probably do?" is *He's an electrician*. Therefore, the correct choice is (C).

Now go on to the first question.

1. Man: I'm looking for the dressings. Do you know where they are?
   Woman: Yes, they're in aisle 6 next to the deli.
   Question: Where does this conversation probably take place? (12 seconds)

2. Man: Do you want me to check under the hood?
   Woman: Yes, please. Could you take a look at the radiator?
   Question: What does the woman imply? (12 seconds)

3. Woman: Did you visit your sister last weekend?
   Man: Well, I intended to, but she called up saying she would be out of town, so I went to San Francisco instead.
   Question: What did the man do last weekend?

4. Man: Ma'am, you were speeding. May I see your driver's license, please?
    Woman: Would my car registration do?
    Question: What does the woman mean? (12 seconds)

5. Man: Good morning. I'd like to speak to Mr. Phillips, please.
    Woman: Mr. Phillips is not at this office today. He's at the Crenshaw Branch. He's there Monday, Wednesday, and Friday this week.
    Question: When will Mr Phillips be at this office? (12 seconds)

6. Man: How much shall I leave him, do you think?
    Woman: It's up to you, Sam, but don't forget we waited ages for those shrimps.
    Question: What will Sam probably do? (12 seconds)

7. Man: Did you go to the concert last night?
    Woman: Well, I had intended to go, but I changed my mind at the last moment.
    Question: What does the man mean? (12 seconds)

8. Woman: You'll love this apartment. It has two bedrooms, a big kitchen, air conditioning, and a wonderful view!
    Man: Yes, it certainly has a fine view and plenty of space, but I have a sleeping problem and it's too near the freeway.
    Question: What is the man implying about the apartment? (12 seconds)

9. Man: I have two tickets for the baseball game tonight. Would you like to come?
    Woman: I'd love to, but I promised my mother I'd take my sister to a show.
    Question: What is the woman going to do tonight? (12 seconds)

10. Man: Could I try some of that delicious ice cream?
    Woman: No, sorry. There's hardly enough for dinner.
    Question: What does the woman mean? (12 seconds)

11. Woman: How would you like your salad - with thousand island, blue cheese, or the special house dressing?
    Man: I don't care for blue cheese, and I always have thousand island, so I'll try the house special.
    Question: What is the woman's occupation? (12 seconds)

12. Woman: How do I look in my new dress?
    Man: It fits you like a glove and matches your eyes perfectly. You look wonderful.
    Question: What does the man mean? (12 seconds)

13. Woman: Are you going to the college dance tomorrow?
    Man: Well, I do have something else lined up.
    Question: What will the man do tomorrow? (12 seconds)

14. Man: When will we have our midterm and final?
    Woman: Your midterm will be in the fifth week, and the final will be at the end of this quarter.
    Question: What is the relationship between the two speakers? (18 seconds)

15. Man: Would you like to join me? I'm going to have a quick snack before my 12 o'clock class.

Woman: I'd like to join you, but my class is earlier.
Question: What will the woman probably do? (12 seconds)

16. Woman: Albert is going to the ballet with Yvette tonight.
     Man: Oh, so she convinced him then.
     Question: What had the man assumed about Albert? (12 seconds)

17. Woman: Should I call Leon and tell him we'll be late?
     Man: I don't think so. He's probably already waiting for us outside.
     Question: What does the man mean? (12 seconds)

18. Man: Do you think you'll ever understand these essays in philosophy?
     Woman: Sure, if I live to be hundred.
     Question: What is the woman implying? (12 seconds)

19. Man: Martha said the biology final is going to be easy.
     Woman: How does she know that?
     Question: What does the woman want to know? (12 seconds)

20. Woman: Peter sure knows what he's doing when it comes to fixing cars.
     Man: That's not the way I see it.
     Question: What does the man mean? (12 seconds)

21. Man: What seems to be the problem?
     Woman: I'm not sure, except that my tapes keep getting stuck. You might have to replace a part on this recorder.
     Question: What is the relationship between the two speakers? (12 seconds)

22. Woman: Look at this beautiful little electric car. It would be a nice present for your niece.
     Man: Sure, if I owned a national bank.
     Question: What is the man implying? (12 seconds)

23. Woman: I'm driving to Pasadena tomorrow to watch the Rose Bowl Parade.
     Man: Why would you want to do that when it's going to be on TV?
     Question: What does the man want to know? (12 seconds)

24. Man: Evelyn wasn't in our Asian history class today, so she missed taking her final.
     Woman: On the contrary, she took it early because she knew she had to go out of town.
     Question: What does the woman mean? (12 seconds)

25. Man: Did you hear that Tracy was accepted at Stanford?
     Woman: So, she did apply after all.
     Question: What did the woman assume about Tracy? (12 seconds)

26. Man: Could you work this vase on my potter's wheel while I go check the oven?
     Woman: I would, but I've got this bowl to mold while it's still wet.
     Question: What is the woman saying? (12 seconds)

27. Man: I hear that Rene got a good grade because of you.
     Woman: Yes, I bent over backwards to help him pass the test.
     Question: What is the woman saying? (12 seconds)

28. Woman: I'm thinking seriously of buying a new computer this month.
     Man: I'd wait a while if I were you. I just read that some new high-powered models
               will be on the market by June.
     Question: What is the man suggesting? (12 seconds)

29. Man: Let's go to the fashion show that the student designers are having on Saturday.
     Woman: I'd love to, but I'm going to the art museum.
     Question: What is the woman saying? (12 seconds)

30. Woman: I was very disappointed with the election results last Thursday.
     Man: So was I. Do you know, every candidate I voted for lost!
     Question: What does the man mean? (12 seconds)

This is the end of Part A.

Part B

Directions: In this part, you will hear longer conversations. After each conversation, you will be asked
several questions. You will hear the conversations and the questions about them only one time. They
will not be repeated. Therefore, you must listen carefully to understand what each speaker says.

   After you hear a question, read the four possible answers in your test book and choose which
one is the best answer to the question you heard. Then, on your answer sheet, find the number of
the question and fill in the space that corresponds to the letter of the answer you have chosen.

   Remember, you should not take notes or write on your test paper.

Now let us begin Part B with the first conversation.

Questions 31 through 34. Listen to the conversation between two students.
     Man: Melissa, where have you been? I've been waiting 30 minutes.
     Woman: I'm sorry, but I had to finish my lab experiment or I'd get an incomplete grade.
     Man: Oh, I see. Well, we'd better get started on this presentation or we'll get an F!
     Woman: Did you find the old navigation charts?
     Man: No, I haven't been able to find any books on the early explorers that contain old
               maps and charts.
     Woman: We'll have to ask the research librarian then.
     Man: Yes, she's very helpful.
     Woman: I found a model of an old clipper ship in Mr. Mooney's antique shop. He said
               he'd let us use it if we promise to be careful.
     Man: Great! And I've started gathering some of the information we need for our handouts.
     Woman: All right. Well, things aren't going so bad after all!

31. What are these people primarily discussing? (12 seconds)

32. Where is this conversation probably taking place? (12 seconds)

33. What is the man's attitude toward the research librarian? (12 seconds)

34. For what class are the man and woman probably doing their presentation? (12 seconds)

Questions 35 through 38. Listen to the phone conversation between a student and the registrar.

Woman: Hello, Glenville College.
Man: Do you have a course on Managerial Studies at about 8:00?
Woman: Yes, sir, there are courses on Managerial Studies every day from 8:30 a.m., but I'm sorry, all courses are full for this semester. The Policy Studies course is still open, and that's in the afternoon.
Man: No, the afternoon's impossible. Could you check the morning courses again?
Woman: One moment. Yes, sir, there's been a drop in Managerial Studies. You can sign up for that course tomorrow morning.
Man: Fine. Now, is there a course in Sociology in the evening?
Woman: There are courses at 6:30 p.m. on Monday and Wednesday, at 7:30 p.m. on Tuesday and Thursday. There's also a Social Science course on Friday.
Man: OK, I can make the 7:30 class.
Woman: That class is still open. You can register when you come in. Please come in thirty minutes before class to pick up the registration forms.

35. What is the purpose of the phone call? (12 seconds)

36. When does this conversation take place? (12 seconds)

37. What is the woman's attitude toward the man? (12 seconds)

38. What evening course does the man choose? (12 seconds)

This is the end of Part B.

Part C

Directions: In this part, you will hear various talks. After each talk, you will be asked several questions. The talks and questions will not be repeated. They will not be written out for you. Therefore, you must listen carefully to understand what the speaker says.

After you hear a question, read the four possible answers in your test book and choose which one is the best answer to the question you heard. Then, on your answer sheet, find the number of the question and fill in the space that corresponds to the letter of the answer you have chosen.

Listen to this sample talk.
You will hear: **The National Health Research Center, perhaps more than any other organization, will directly affect the lives of millions of Americans every day. The Health Research Center volunteers will work all over the United States to provide information on diet and lifestyles. The bulk of the foundation's time will be spent conducting seminars and distributing pamphlets on how to prevent major illness and increase longevity. A free long-distance 800 number is available for anyone with health-related questions.**

Now listen to the following question.

What is the speaker's purpose?

You will read: (A) To get you to join the foundation.
(B) To inform you of the existence of the Health Research Center.
(C) To persuade you to give a donation to the foundation.
(D) To ask you to distribute pamphlets for the foundation.

The best answer to the question, "What is the speaker's purpose?" is *To inform you of the existence of the Health Research Center.* Therefore, you should choose answer (B).

Now listen to the next example.

Why would you use the center's 800 number?

You will read: (A) To volunteer to distribute pamphlets.
                  (B) To make a contribution to the Health Research Center.
                  (C) To obtain a schedule of seminars.
                  (D) To ask questions regarding good health.

The best answer to the question. "Why would you use the center's 800 number?" is *To ask questions regarding good health.* Therefore, you should choose answer (D).

Now let us begin Part C with the first talk.

Questions 39 through 42.

A rare fossil of an ancient "crab" recently discovered in South Carolina has many geologists convinced that part of the Southeastern United States was once African or European soil. Sara Samson, a graduate student of the University of South Carolina, stumbled upon the fossil on a field trip. The particular type of crab-like creature that she found lived 500 million years ago and is, according to geologists, definitely not American. For years, geologists have argued about whether or not the Carolina Slate belt, which runs from Alabama to Eastern Virginia, represents foreign soil picked up when continents collided and then separated 400 million years ago. Samson's find, along with others discovered at the site, convinced even the sceptics. These fossils are the first hard evidence that a piece of Africa or Europe was left behind when the continents collided. Geologists now hope to match these fossils with others found in Africa, France, or Spain.

39. What is the main topic of this talk? (12 seconds)

40. Where was the fossil found? (12 seconds)

41 According to the lecture, what happened when the continents collided? (12 seconds)

42. According to the lecture, how are geologists reacting to the discovery of the fossil? (12 seconds)

Questions 43 through 45.

I'd like to welcome all of you to the Western Heritage Museum. Before going into the exhibit rooms, I'd like to point out our authentic overland stagecoach. The overland stage played an important part in the history of the American West. In 1858, the first overland stage crossed America from east to west. From that point on, it became the most popular means of carrying people, mail, and baggage across the land. Loaded with passengers and cargo, the overland stage rode along at an average speed of eight miles an hour, following the rough trails made earlier by the wagon trains. As romantic as the movies and television have shown the overland stage to be, this adventure into the unknown was full of discomfort and problems. Illness, blizzards, bandits, unfriendly natives, mechanical problems, and accidents turned many a dream trip into a nightmare. The first stagecoaches were especially unstable and uncomfortable, but soon the Concord coach was built, a sturdy vehicle with a special design that made the ride easier. It stood eight feet high and could accommodate as many as 21 passengers, nine seated inside on three benches and a dozen more on the roof.

43. What does the speaker mainly talk about? (12 seconds)

44. According to the lecture, passengers had to endure all of the following problems EXCEPT . . . (12 seconds)

45. What is the speaker's attitude toward the historical importance of the stagecoach? (12 seconds)

Questions 46 through 50.

Heart disease typically strikes people in their forties or fifties. But there is now evidence that the malady can sometimes be traced to the early habits of childhood. The American Heart Association states that the arteries of American infants and children can accumulate fatty plaque, the principal promoter of heart disease. For that reason, they have recently recommended dietary restrictions for children two years or older. Restrictions include limiting the intake of fat, salt, and most important, cholesterol. The new focus on children's diets started when the American Heart Association considered statistical studies showing that U.S. children have higher blood-cholesterol concentrations than do children of other populations. A prudent diet during childhood, the Association concludes, will reduce the risk of heart attack throughout life.

46. What is the main topic of the talk? (12 seconds)

47. What is the purpose of this talk? (12 seconds)

48. According to the talk, which group does heart disease generally attack? (12 seconds)

49. According to the talk, which restriction in children's diets is most effective? (12 seconds)

50. According to the talk, what is thought to be the main cause of heart disease? (12 seconds)

Stop work on Section 1.

Practice Test 2

LISTENING COMPREHENSION

In this section of the test, you will have an opportunity to demonstrate your ability to understand conversations and talks in English. In this section, there are answers to all the questions based on the information heard.

Part A

<u>Directions:</u> In Part A, you will hear short conversations between two people. At the end of each conversation, you will hear a question about the conversation. The conversation and question will not be repeated. Therefore, you must listen carefully to understand what each speaker says. After you hear a question, read the four possible answers in your test book and choose the best answer to the question you heard. Then, on your answer sheet, find the number of the question and fill in the space that corresponds to the letter of the answer you have chosen

Listen to an example on the recording:

Man: **What seems to be the problem, ma'am?**
Woman: **Well, the light switch is broken and a plug needs repairing.**
Question: **What kind of work does the man probably do?**

In your book you will read: (A) He's a carpenter.
(B) He's a plumber.
(C) He's an electrician.
(D) He's an engineer.

From the conversation, you learn that the light switch is broken and a plug needs repairing. The best answer to the question, "What kind of work does the man probably do?" is *He's an electrician*. Therefore, the correct choice is (C).

Now go on to the first question.

1. Man: How was your trip to Chicago?
    Woman: To tell the truth, I would rather have spent my vacation here.
    Question: What does the man imply? (12 seconds)

2. Man: Let's go for a walk.
    Woman: I'd like to, but I feel a bit under the weather.
    Question: What does the woman mean? (12 seconds)

3. Man: Will that be cash or account charge?
    Woman: Can I write a check?
    Question: What is the woman asking? (12 seconds)

4. Woman: Do you want to leave for class immediately?
    Man: I still have to finish my paper.
    Question: What is the woman asking? (12 seconds)

5. Woman: Do you prefer tea or coffee after lunch?
    Man: I don't care for tea that much, and I only drink coffee in the evening.
    Question: What can be inferred about the man?

6. Man: Where have you been? I thought I was going to take the plane without you.
    Woman: I'm sorry. I was waiting for you in front of the check-in. Luckily, I thought of coming to the departure gate.
    Question: Where had the woman assumed they would meet?

7. Man: Cheryl seems to have put on a lot of weight recently.
    Woman: Yes, she's not been going to the gymnasium so regularly.
    Question: What does the woman mean? (12 seconds)

8. Man: This cake's delicious! Did you make it yourself?
    Woman: You must be kidding. My sister got it from the bakery.
    Question: What does the woman imply? (12 seconds)

9. Man: You don't think much of Jack, do you?
    Woman: You can say that again!
    Question: What does the woman mean? (12 seconds)

10. Man: Betty is always complaining about her son.
    Woman: She should take care of my three teenage boys and see what it's like.
    Question: What does the woman mean? (12 seconds)

11. Woman: If I don't get some money from my parents by Friday, could I borrow some from you?
    Man: By all means!
    Question: What does the man mean? (12 seconds)

12. Man: Could you check my balance, please?
    Woman: Just a minute. I'll look it up.
    Question: Where is this conversation probably taking place? (12 seconds)

13. Woman: I'm swamped. I'll never be able to get through these assignments by Friday!
    Man: I thought I was the only one!
    Question: What does the man mean? (12 seconds)

14. Woman: I'm wondering about the fabric of this dress. Is it washable? I don't want to run up a big cleaning bill.
    Man: All the dresses in this section are polyester, so you shouldn't have a problem.
    Question: What does the man imply? (12 seconds)

15. Man: You've done this before, right?
    Woman: No, but if we follow the directions precisely, we shouldn't have any trouble.
    Question: What does the woman think they should do? (12 seconds)

16. Woman: You need to sign for this special delivery package.
    Man: Do you have a pen?
    Question: What is the woman's probable occupation?

17. Man: If I were you, I'd leave early today. I hear the holiday traffic is already building up.
    Woman: Sounds like a good idea.
    Question: What does the man suggest the woman do? (12 seconds)

18. Man: Would you like me to hold those items for you while you continue shopping?
    Woman: Thanks, but that won't be necessary.
    Question: What does the man offer to do for the woman? (12 seconds)

19. Woman: Can you tell me where the Egyptian art exhibit is located?
    Man: Yes, of course. It's on the second floor, in the east wing.
    Question: What is the relationship between the two speakers? (12 seconds)

20. Man: Well, what did you think?
    Woman: I loved it, but I can hardly hear you because my ears are still ringing!
    Question: When did this conversation take place?

21. Man: That was the most boring book I've ever read.
    Woman: How can you say that?
    Question: What does the woman want to know? (12 seconds)

22. Woman: I see you're eating a salad for lunch again today.
    Man: Yes, but I've had just about enough of this diet.
    Question: What is the man implying? (12 seconds)

23. Man: New Hampshire's Mt. Washington is the most famous mountain in America.
    Woman: I beg to differ, but that reputation belongs to Pike's Peak in Colorado.
    Question: What is the woman saying? (12 seconds)

24. Man: I have three term papers due on Friday, and I haven't started one of them yet.
    Woman: I don't believe it!
    Question: What is the woman saying? (12 seconds)

25. Man: Why don't we stop by the gym today? I hear they've got some new equipment.
    Woman: Thanks, but I've already seen it.
    Question: What does the man want to do? (12 seconds)

26. Woman: I've decided to start writing children's books.
    Man: Oh, so you're not going to teach any more then?
    Question: What is the man assuming? (12 seconds)

27. Man: Don't you think that Professor Peterson is giving us too many papers to write?
    Woman: I don't think so. Writing is one of the best ways I know to learn a subject.
    Question: What is the woman saying? (12 seconds)

28. Man: What do you suggest I do?
    Woman: Well, I think you should sell off a few of these stocks and buy mutual funds, maybe even get into the bond market.
    Question: What is the woman's probable occupation. (12 seconds)

29. Man: Would you like me to check on that book you ordered?
    Woman: Why, yes, thank you. I'd almost forgotten about it.That's OK.
    Question: What is the man offering to do? (12 seconds)

30. Man: Acupuncture is based on the principle that in all diseases there are tender areas at certain points on the body that disappear when the disease is cured.
    Woman: That's OK, but how does acupuncture actually work?
    Question: What does the woman want to know? (12 seconds)

This is the end of Part A.

Part B

Directions: In this part, you will hear longer conversations. After each conversation, you will be asked several questions. You will hear the conversations and the questions about them only one time. They will not be repeated. Therefore, you must listen carefully to understand what each speaker says.

After you hear a question, read the four possible answers in your test book and choose which one is the best answer to the question you heard. Then, on your answer sheet, find the number of the question and fill in the space that corresponds to the letter of the answer you have chosen.

Remember, you should not take notes or write on your test paper.

Now let us begin Part B with the first conversation.

Questions 31 through 35. Listen to the conversation about a Los Angeles attraction.
    Woman: Have you ever visited the La Brea tar pits next to the Los Angeles County Museum? Someone told me they have specimens of prehistoric animals that were actually found right here in L.A.!
    Man: I've only seen pictures of prehistoric animals. I've never seen any actual remains. How did they get there?
    Woman: Well, they found the bones of these animals in the tar. Some of them are actually 40,000 years old.
    Man: But how were they preserved for so long?
    Woman: What happened was that the deep tar pits became covered with water and when the animals went to drink from the pools, they were caught in the sticky tar.
    Man: When did they first discover the bones?
    Woman: Well, the Spanish who settled in Los Angeles used the asphalt in the pits for roofing their houses, but they threw away any bones they found. Later, when engineers were drilling for oil in the area, they found the bones again. Finally a scientist with an oil company discovered they were from prehistoric animals. But archeologists really started digging up the bones from about 1906.
    Man: What kind of animals do these bones belong to?
    Woman: Well, there was the great lion, and hundreds of saber-toothed tigers, both of which became extinct when the other animals disappeared . . . oh, and giant sloths that hung upside down in the trees. Then they found the skulls of giant buffaloes, and horses much like the ones we have today, but they are all extinct now, of course.
    Man: Come on. Let's see all this.

31. What is the main subject of the conversation? (12 seconds)

32. According to the conversation, why were prehistoric animal bones found in the tar pits? (12 seconds)

33. According to the conversation, how were the bones preserved? (12 seconds)

34. Who discovered the bones were prehistoric? (12 seconds)

35. What will the man and woman probably do? (12 seconds)

Questions 36 through 38. Listen to the conversation about music.

Man:	What a surprise to see you here. What bus are you taking?
Woman:	Number 35.
Man:	That's the bus to Monterey. Are you going to the Jazz Festival?
Woman:	Yes, I am.
Man:	I didn't know you were a jazz fan.
Woman:	Well, I am.
Man:	But I thought you played with a rock-and-roll group.
Woman:	I do, but I still love jazz. If you listened to our music, you'd know that we use jazz sounds in our work.
Man:	Really? Well, that's very interesting. Who's your favorite jazz musician?
Woman:	Louis Armstrong, of course.
Man:	Why?
Woman:	He had a worldwide impact on jazz. He came from a very poor background and with talent and determination, he became the greatest jazz artist of his time.
Man:	He was famous for his extraordinary ability to improvise.
Woman:	Yes. He could invent sounds as he went along and transform ordinary tunes into sweeping melodies. He was the greatest that ever lived.
Man:	I couldn't agree with you more.

36. What are these people primarily discussing? (12 seconds)

37. What do the speakers have in common? (12 seconds)

38. According to the conversation, what was Louis Armstrong well known for? (12 seconds)

This is the end of Part B.

Part C

Directions: In this part, you will hear various talks. After each talk, you will be asked several questions. The talks and questions will not be repeated. They will not be written out for you. Therefore, you must listen carefully to understand what the speaker says.

After you hear a question, read the four possible answers in your test book and choose which one is the best answer to the question you heard. Then, on your answer sheet, find the number of the question and fill in the space that corresponds to the letter of the answer you have chosen.

Listen to this sample talk.

You will hear: **The National Health Research Center, perhaps more than any other organization, will directly affect the lives of millions of Americans every day. The Health Research Center volunteers will work all over the United States to provide information on diet and lifestyles. The bulk of thc foundation's time will be spent conducting seminars and distributing pamphlets on how to prevent major illness and increase longevity. A free long-distance 800 number is available for anyone with health-related questions.**

Now listen to the following question.

What is the speaker's purpose?

You will read: (A)   To get you to join the foundation.
                    (B)   To inform you of the existence of the Health Research Center.
                    (C)   To persuade you to give a donation to the foundation.
                    (D)   To ask you to distribute pamphlets for the foundation.

The best answer to the question, "What is the speaker's purpose?" is *To inform you of the existence of the Health Research Center.* Therefore, you should choose answer (B).

Now listen to the next example.

Why would you use the center's 800 number?

You will read: (A)   To volunteer to distribute pamphlets.
                    (B)   To make a contribution to the Health Research Center.
                    (C)   To obtain a schedule of seminars.
                    (D)   To ask questions regarding good health.

The best answer to the question. "Why would you use the center's 800 number?" is *To ask questions regarding good health.* Therefore, you should choose answer (D).

Now let us begin Part C with the first talk.

Questions 39 through 42

Nathaniel Hawthorne wrote strange and somber stories with many layers of meaning. In creating his novels, he drew deeply on the past, especially the Puritan religious inheritance of New England. Hawthorne was born in Salem, Massachusetts, in 1804. His father, a sea captain, died when he was just four. Hawthorne was a quiet, solitary boy, happiest in the company of books and his own thoughts. After leaving college in Maine in 1825, he shut himself away for 12 years in an attic room of his mother's old house in Salem, determined to become a writer. He produced one novel, *Fanshawe,* and a number of short stories. From 1839, he worked for several years as a customs agent official in Boston. Then, in 1850, he published his first great novel, *The Scarlet Letter.* It is concerned with prejudice, passion, and guilt in 17th-century New England. The book brought him widespread recognition. *The House of the Seven Gables* and *The Blithedale Romance* quickly followed. From 1853 to 1857, Hawthorne was the U.S. consul in Liverpool, England. Afterward, he lived in Italy for two years. His last completed novel, *The Marble Faun,* was set in Rome. He died in New England in 1864.

136

39. What is the main topic of the lecture? (12 seconds)

40. In what course was this lecture probably given? (12 seconds)

41. According to the lecture, *The Scarlet Letter* was NOT concerned with . . . (12 seconds)

42. It can be inferred from the lecture that Hawthorne . . . (12 seconds)

Questions 43 through 45.
Good morning, students. Today we will continue our investigation of the mosquito. We all thought that mosquitoes follow skin odors, but no such odor has been identified. It turns out, in fact, that no skin seems to be as attractive to a mosquito as a current of air having the right degree of warmth and humidity. But a mosquito can be turned off its course by a repellent. This is how it works. A mosquito senses humidity in an airstream by means of tiny pores in the hairs located on its antennae. These hairs send electrical impulses to the central nervous system whenever they encounter humidity in the air. The repellent blocks the pores through which mosquitoes sense the presence of water vapor in the air. As a mosquito comes in for a landing on a warm moist body, the repellent blocks the mosquito's sensors, and realizing it has lost its moist current of air, it instinctively changes its course.

43. According to the speaker, what are mosquitoes attracted to? (12 seconds)

44. What happens when the mosquito comes into contact with the repellent? (12 seconds)

45. According to the talk, what can be inferred about mosquito repellents? (12 seconds)

Questions 46 through 50.
Before we leave, I'll be checking to make sure everyone has the proper gear and clothing. Sudden changes in temperature and weather conditions can take place as we increase our elevation. Although it's warm here, we can expect wind, cold, and damp and chilly fogs at the summit. I don't want to frighten you, but some 50 people are known to have died while attempting this rigorous climb. Most cases resulted from a lack of proper preparation. That's why you were all given a checklist, which we'll review in a moment. The hike to the summit will take approximately five hours. Most of the way will be through pine forest until we reach the timberline at 4,500 feet, when the trees will end and only a few low bushes and arctic wild flowers will be present. From the top we'll be able to see into Canada and view other mountain peaks in this area.

46. What is the purpose of the talk? (12 seconds)

47. What is the speaker's probable occupation? (12 seconds)

48. Where was the talk probably given? (12 seconds)

49. What does the speaker imply about weather conditions high on the mountain? (12 seconds)

50. According to the talk, what kind of landscape can be expected at the summit? (12 seconds)

Stop work on Section 1.

Practice Test 3

LISTENING COMPREHENSION

In this section of the test, you will have an opportunity to demonstrate your ability to understand conversations and talks in English. In this section, there are answers to all the questions based on the information heard.

Part A

<u>Directions:</u> In Part A, you will hear short conversations between two people. At the end of each conversation, you will hear a question about the conversation. The conversation and question will not be repeated. Therefore, you must listen carefully to understand what each speaker says. After you hear a question, read the four possible answers in your test book and choose the best answer to the question you heard. Then, on your answer sheet, find the number of the question and fill in the space that corresponds to the letter of the answer you have chosen

Listen to an example on the recording:

Man:	**What seems to be the problem, ma'am?**
Woman:	**Well, the light switch is broken and a plug needs repairing.**
Question:	**What kind of work does the man probably do?**

In your book you will read: (A) He's a carpenter.
(B) He's a plumber.
(C) He's an electrician.
(D) He's an engineer.

From the conversation, you learn that the light switch is broken and a plug needs repairing. The best answer to the question, "What kind of work does the man probably do?" is *He's an electrician.* Therefore, the correct choice is (C).

Now go on to the first question.

1. Man: Looks like you've got a lot of reading to do.
    Woman: And that's just for my philosophy class!
    Question: What does the woman imply? (12 seconds)

2. Woman: Patrick is telling everyone he got his engineering degree.
    Man: Yes, but you don't hear him mention how long it took him, do you?
    Question: What is the man saying about Patrick? (12 seconds)

3. Woman: They gave that movie a very bad review on TV last night.
    Man: That's just their opinion.
    Question: What does the man mean? (12 seconds)

4. Man: Where can I find the textbooks for the French 101 course?
    Woman: They'll be in aisle 2 under French.
    Question: Where is this conversation taking place? (12 seconds)

5. Man: My hair is getting so long.
    Woman: Yes, you should have it trimmed.
    Question: What is the woman suggesting? (12 seconds)

6. Woman: Do you like dancing?
    Man: As a rule I do, but frankly I don't go in for these new dances.
    Question: What does the man mean? (12 seconds)

7. Man: These copies aren't coming out too well.
    Woman: Let's try one on a darker print.
    Question: What does the woman advise the man to do? (12 seconds)

8. Man: Would you rather go to the movies or watch T.V. tonight?
    Woman: I'd just as soon turn in early if you don't mind.
    Question: What would the woman rather do? (12 seconds)

9. Woman: Of the two apartments we've just seen, which do you like better?
    Man: The single one was cheaper, no doubt, but the two-bedroom one is bigger and it's
               worth paying the difference.
    Question: What does the man imply? (12 seconds)

10. Woman: Would you like me to make you some coffee?
    Man: Don't bother.
    Question: What does the man mean? (12 seconds)

11. Man: I'd like to thank Mary for her gift. Do you have her address?
    Woman: Sorry, I don't have it on me right now.
    Question: What is the man going to do? (12 seconds)

12. Man: I've had a leaky faucet for a week, and I just can't fix it. Do you happen to know
               a good plumber?
    Woman: Why don't I take a look at it? I'm an old hand at plumbing.
    Question: What does the woman mean? (12 seconds)

13. Man: Have you heard from your brother John recently?
    Woman: Last time I saw him was three months ago when he was going to New York, but
               if there were something wrong he'd call me.
    Question: What can be inferred from the woman's statement? (12 seconds)

14. Woman: Do you think Phil can get a scholarship to Harvard?
    Man: He doesn't stand a chance!
    Question: What does the man mean? (12 seconds)

15. Woman: Can I park my car in your driveway for the night?
    Man: Well, I'll be leaving at the crack of dawn.
    Question: What is the man's problem? (12 seconds)

16. Woman: I didn't see Raymond at the library last night.
    Man: He must have finished his term paper then.
    Question: What had the man assumed about Raymond? (12 seconds)

17. Man: Marge told me you decided not to try out for the play.
    Woman: When did she tell you that?
    Question: What does the woman want to know? (12 seconds)

18. Woman: Please fill this test tube with water and then pour it into the beaker with the blue label.
    Man: OK, but let me turn off this burner first.
    Question: What are these people doing? (12 seconds)

19. Woman: Would you like to come sailing with us on Sunday?
    Man: I'd love to, but I get seasick out there!
    Question: What will the man probably do on Sunday? (12 seconds)

20. Woman: Jacob, I haven't seen you for a week.
    Man: Yes, I've been in the observatory all week studying the comet crashes on Jupiter.
    Question: What is the man's probable occupation? (12 seconds)

21. Man: Gosh, Melinda, that's a pretty heavy schedule you've signed up for.
    Woman: It's a piece of cake compared to the classes I had last semester.
    Question: What does the woman mean? (12 seconds)

22. Woman: Why don't I hold your place in the ticket line while you go buy some popcorn?
    Man: I'd say that a great idea if there weren't even a longer line at the refreshment counter!
    Question: What will the man probably do? (12 seconds)

23. Man: I see you still have your leg in a cast.
    Woman: Yes, and have I learned my lesson.
    Question: What is the woman implying (12 seconds)

24. Man: Would you go outside and tell me if I need a jacket?
    Woman: Sure, I'll do that right now.
    Question: What does the man want the woman to do? (12 seconds)

25. Woman: I just bought myself a stair climbing exercise machine.
    Man: That's terrific. You know, it's good for your heart and tones the lower body too.
    Question: What can be inferred about the woman? (12 seconds)

26. Woman: I have to write a paper on meteorites.
    Man: Why don't you go to the planetarium, Rosey? They have a special exhibit on meteors right now.
    Question: What is the man suggesting? (12 seconds)

27. Man: I'm carrying a B average in Middle Eastern studies.
    Woman: Yes, but you still have your final to take.
    Question: What is the woman saying? (12 seconds)

28. Man: I'm a bit nervous because I've never done this before.
    Woman: Don't worry. I'll hold the reins. Now, put your left foot in the stirrup, grab the horn and lift yourself up.
    Question: What is the man probably doing? (12 seconds)

29. Woman: Why don't you sit in on my 1 o'clock music class today. I think you'll enjoy it.
    Man: I usually have lunch at that time, but this may be well worth a change in schedule.
    Question: What will the man probably do? (12 seconds)

30. Man: Will you be taking any courses during the summer break?
    Woman: Not if I can help it.
    Question: What does the woman mean? (12 seconds)

This is the end of Part A.

Part B

Directions: In this part, you will hear longer conversations. After each conversation, you will be asked several questions. You will hear the conversations and the questions about them only one time. They will not be repeated. Therefore, you must listen carefully to understand what each speaker says. After you hear a question, read the four possible answers in your test book and choose which one is the best answer to the question you heard. Then, on your answer sheet, find the number of the question and fill in the space that corresponds to the letter of the answer you have chosen. Remember, you should not take notes or write on your test paper.

Now let us begin Part B with the first conversation.

Questions 31 through 33. Listen to the following conversation about early mail delivery.
    Woman: I just saw a movie in which they mentioned the Pony Express. What do you know about it?
    Man: It was one of the legends of the West. They were the riders who delivered mail on horseback from one end of the country to the other.
    Woman: It must have taken them months.
    Man: Before the Pony Express, it took from one to six months for mail to be delivered across country, but the Pony Express only took ten days.
    Woman: That's quite an improvement, but it still doesn't seem like a very reliable method of delivering mail. What if something went wrong?
    Man: Well, there were many obstacles that each rider had to face, such as storms, deserts to cross, Indians and so on, but out of the 80 riders, only one died, and his horse survived to get to the next station with the mail intact! Each rider rode an average of 75 miles a day and they changed horses every 10 to 12 miles.
    Woman: It seems incredible! How long did the Pony Express last?
    Man: Believe or it not, it only lasted 18 months. It was only a week from the start of telegraph communication that it ended. It seems a shame somehow, doesn't it?

31. What was the Pony Express? (12 seconds)

32. According to the conversation, did the mail get to its destination every time? (12 seconds)

33. When did the Pony Express come to an end? (12 seconds)

Questions 34 through 38. Listen to the conversation about sounds.

Woman:	Jack, you haven't heard a word any of us have said. Get those earphones off your head!
Man:	I'm sorry. I was listening to something called "Sounds of the Deep."
Woman:	Is that a new rock group?
Man:	No, no. It's a recording of sounds from the ocean.
Woman:	Sounds? I thought the sea was called "The Silent World."
Man:	Well, it used to be called that. But now we know that sea-dwelling animals make all kind of sounds.
Woman:	Like a barking dog?
Man:	Something like that. A humpback whale's song can be heard by other whales hundreds of miles away.
Woman:	How do scientists record these sounds?
Man:	They use underwater microphones, called hydrophones.
Woman:	What kinds of sounds to the animals make?
Man:	Well, whales and dolphins make whistling and clicking noises. Many fish make a drumming sound by moving a special muscle. Some animals, like crabs and lobsters, make rubbing or clapping sounds.
Woman:	Really. I never knew that. I'd like to listen to that recording if you don't mind.
Man:	Sure, here. Put on these earphones. Everyone can take their turn if they'd like.

34. What is the main topic of this conversation? (12 seconds)

35. How does the woman feel about what the man is telling her? (12 seconds)

36. What can be inferred about sea-dwelling mammals? (12 seconds)

37. According to the man, what do scientists use to record underwater sounds? (12 seconds)

38. According to the man, what kind of sounds do crabs and lobsters make? (12 seconds)

This is the end of Part B.

Part C

Directions: In this part, you will hear various talks. After each talk, you will be asked several questions. The talks and questions will not be repeated. They will not be written out for you. Therefore, you must listen carefully to understand what the speaker says.

After you hear a question, read the four possible answers in your test book and choose which one is the best answer to the question you heard. Then, on your answer sheet, find the number of the question and fill in the space that corresponds to the letter of the answer you have chosen.

Listen to this sample talk.

You will hear: **The National Health Research Center, perhaps more than any other organization, will directly affect the lives of millions of Americans every day. The Health Research Center volunteers will work all over the United States to provide information on diet and lifestyles. The bulk of the foundation's time will be spent conducting seminars and distributing pamphlets on how to prevent major illness and increase longevity. A free long-distance 800 number is available for anyone with health-related questions.**

Now listen to the following question.

What is the speaker's purpose?

You will read: (A) To get you to join the foundation.
(B) To inform you of the existence of the Health Research Center.
(C) To persuade you to give a donation to the foundation.
(D) To ask you to distribute pamphlets for the foundation.

The best answer to the question, "What is the speaker's purpose?" is *To inform you of the existence of the Health Research Center.* Therefore, you should choose answer (B).

Now listen to the next example.

Why would you use the center's 800 number?

You will read: (A) To volunteer to distribute pamphlets.
(B) To make a contribution to the Health Research Center.
(C) To obtain a schedule of seminars.
(D) To ask questions regarding good health.

The best answer to the question. "Why would you use the center's 800 number?" is *To ask questions regarding good health.* Therefore, you should choose answer (D).

Now let us begin Part C with the first talk.

Questions 39 through 41.

I'm happy to see so many of you gathered around our crocodile pool. I've studied them more than any other of our animals. Did you know that crocodiles are closely related to dinosaurs? Their bones show us that they have the same skull structure and their teeth grow in a similar way. Like almost all dinosaurs, crocodiles have much bigger hind legs than front legs and are protected by bony armor. Although dinosaurs were mainly land-living creatures, the crocodiles took to the water, which is where we still find them. Many of the early crocodiles lived in the sea. Their feet were paddle-like, and their tail ended in a fish-like fin. Today, most crocodiles and their relatives live beside rivers or lakes. They swim using their large flattened tails, but often float gently up to their prey, with only their nostrils above the water. A crocodile is able to grab and hold a struggling animal underwater because, as it breathes, air flows into a separate channel above its mouth and into its throat. All living crocodiles hatch from eggs, which are usually laid in a nest close to the water. The female stays nearby. When she hears squeaks from inside the eggs, she uncovers them and, in some cases, carries the babies to the water in her mouth.

39. What is the main topic of this talk? (12 seconds)

40. Where was this talk probably given? (12 seconds)

41. According to the talk, crocodiles are similar to dinosaurs in all of the following ways EXCEPT . . . (12 seconds)

Questions 42 through 45.

This afternoon I should like to talk about an interesting aspect of animal behavior. Do you know why salmon return to spawn in the stream where they were first hatched? Well, we now believe that this is because of a phenomenon that biologists call imprinting. Let me give you an example. Many kinds of birds treat the first moving object they see as their mother. Of course, in fact, the first moving object they generally see is their mother, but during the first few hours of life a bird will imprint on almost anything. They will accept foster mothers of their own species, or adults of another species or even mechanical or inanimate objects. Even color, shape, and motion does not seem to be essential. They will just imprint on any object that contrasts with the environment.

This process is not limited to birds but occurs in mammals as well. Imprinting, in fact, has been extended beyond the original "mother figure." If we return to our question at the beginning of the talk, we can see that the salmon returning to the home stream after years in the ocean can be attributed to a form of imprinting. It is believed that the salmon's behavior is the result of imprinting of the stream odor on the newly hatched fish. They then seek out the stream odor on their return to fresh water and rarely end up in the wrong stream.

42. What is the main topic of this lecture? (12 seconds)

43. In which course was this lecture probably given? (12 seconds)

44. According to the lecture, what is essential when young birds imprint? (12 seconds)

45. How does imprinting affect the salmon? (12 seconds)

Questions 46 through 50.
Any information about materials prior to 1981 can be found in the card catalogue. Access is possible by author, title, series, and subject, and the call number is in the upper left-hand corner. When the item you want is not on the shelf, you should ask for help at the circulation counter. Staff will check the hold shelf, material to be shelved, and the circulation file. If the title is checked out, you can place a hold on it or ask that it be recalled for you. If the title is not checked out, you can request that a search be made. You will be notified by mail of the results of the search. Searches for periodicals and microfilms must be approved at the Reference Desk. If the title is lost, students and staff can request that it be borrowed through the University Interlibrary Loan Service.

46. Where is the talk probably taking place? (12 seconds)

47. What is the speaker's tone? (12 seconds)

48. According to the talk, what is the first thing you should do if the item you want is not on the shelf? (12 seconds)

49. What does the speaker suggest you do if a missing title is not checked out? (12 seconds)

50. From the talk, what can be inferred about the staff? (12 seconds)

Stop work on Section 1.

Practice Test 4

LISTENING COMPREHENSION

In this section of the test, you will have an opportunity to demonstrate your ability to understand conversations and talks in English. In this section, there are answers to all the questions based on the information heard.

Part A

<u>Directions:</u> In Part A, you will hear short conversations between two people. At the end of each conversation, you will hear a question about the conversation. The conversation and question will not be repeated. Therefore, you must listen carefully to understand what each speaker says. After you hear a question, read the four possible answers in your test book and choose the best answer to the question you heard. Then, on your answer sheet, find the number of the question and fill in the space that corresponds to the letter of the answer you have chosen.

Listen to an example on the recording:

Man:	**What seems to be the problem, ma'am?**
Woman:	**Well, the light switch is broken and a plug needs repairing.**
Question:	**What kind of work does the man probably do?**

In your book you will read:
(A) He's a carpenter.
(B) He's a plumber.
(C) He's an electrician.
(D) He's an engineer.

From the conversation, you learn that the light switch is broken and a plug needs repairing. The best answer to the question, "What kind of work does the man probably do?" is *He's an electrician*. Therefore, the correct choice is (C).

Now go on to the first question.

1. Woman: Jack failed his examination again.
   Man: That's not surprising.
   Question: What does the man imply? (12 seconds)

2. Man: Are we going to Grant's party tonight?
   Woman: Frankly, I don't feel up to it.
   Question: What does the woman mean? (12 seconds)

3. Woman: What did you think of Jerry's presentation?
   Man: It was interesting, but he was really uncomfortable in front of the class.
   Question: What does the man say about Jerry? (12 seconds)

4. Woman: What time does the bus leave?
    Man: On the hour and on the half hour.
    Question: What does the man mean? (12 seconds)

5. Woman: Have you any idea what Jake Johnson's doing these days?
    Man: You know, I lost track of him.
    Question: What does the man mean? (12 seconds)

6. Woman: I'm thinking of dropping my economics class. It's really too difficult for me.
    Man: I know how you feel, but I'd sweat it out for another couple of weeks if I were you. I'm glad I did. The worst part's over anyway.
    Question: What does the man advise the woman to do? (12 seconds)

7. Man: Which exit is for Hollywood Park?
    Woman: It's the next one, so you'd better get in the right lane.
    Question: Where is this conversation taking place? (12 seconds)

8. Man: Do you have any tickets for the play on Saturday? But I don't want to pay a lot.
    Woman: The matinee's sold out. We have some expensive orchestra seats left for the evening performance – your only other choice is the HOT TIX, two and a half hours before the performance.
    Question: What will the man probably do? (12 seconds)

9. Woman: Bob is really doing well. He's become champ of the school team.
    Man: I admit he's the best, but the whole thing has gone to his head.
    Question: What does the man think about Bob? (12 seconds)

10. Woman: Excuse me, do you know where you register for this quarter?
    Man: For registration, go to the administration building, which is right next to the library. You can see the line from here.
    Question: What is the woman? (12 seconds)

11. Man: You know how to apply for a scholarship, don't you?
    Woman: I've never applied for one. Why don't you ask George? He knows the ropes better than I do.
    Question: What does the woman mean? (12 seconds)

12. Woman: Let's go hiking in a National Park over the spring holiday.
    Man: I had planned on doing that myself.
    Question: What will the man do? (12 seconds)

13. Woman: If you don't like to read fiction, do you enjoy reading nonfiction then?
    Man: It's so rare that I have the time to read for pleasure.
    Question: What does the man mean? (12 seconds)

14. Woman: Look, it's Thursday today, and the gallery's still closed!
    Man: Really? Then it didn't open the day before yesterday.
    Question: When did the man assume the gallery should have opened? (12 seconds)

15. Man: That was rather tricky. I thought we'd have trouble.
    Woman: You certainly handled it well.
    Question: What does the woman mean? (12 seconds)

16. Man: Can I help you find something?
    Woman: No, thank you. I'm just browsing.
    Question: What is the woman saying? (12 seconds)

17. Woman: I've never seen Jeremy so happy as he has been since his promotion.
    Man: Well, who wouldn't be? He's making a fortune!
    Question: What does the man mean? (12 seconds)

18. Woman: Edward, I've noticed the long hours you've been working lately. I think you deserve a day off.
    Man: Thank you, Ms. Rogers. I have been working pretty hard lately. I could use a little rest.
    Question: What is the relationship between the two speakers? (12 seconds)

19. Man: I think Ben Hayden is the best candidate for Senator on the November ballot.
    Woman: You must be joking.
    Question: What will the woman probably do? (12 seconds)

20. Man: Have you decided which classes to take next semester?
    Woman: If I had, I'd be registering right now.
    Question: What does the woman imply? (12 seconds)

21. Man: I'm confused about when exactly I should come in.
    Woman: We'll begin slowly, just the violin, then the cello, then the piano. Watch my signal for your first note.
    Question: What is the probable relationship between the two speakers? (12 seconds)

22. Man: Although the grizzly bear can be fierce, there's no more dangerous a mammal than the polar bear.
    Woman: Isn't that the truth!
    Question: What does the woman mean? (12 seconds)

23. Man: I'm not doing very well in French.
    Woman: Why don't you spend extra time in the language lab after school, Ernest? That's what I do.
    Question: What is the woman suggesting? (12 seconds)

24. Man: I can't believe it. I've already spent most of my paycheck at the school bookstore.
    Woman: Yes, and that's only the beginning.
    Question: What is the woman implying? (12 seconds)

25. Woman: Guess what? My recital has been canceled because of the flu epidemic.
    Man: In that case, Winnie, you must be very pleased.
    Question: What has the man assumed? (12 seconds)

26. Man: I'm sorry we're late, Donna. What a time we had getting here.
    Woman: That's all right. The important thing is that you're safe.
    Question: What is the man saying? (12 seconds)

27. Man: I'll be so glad when I don't have to take any more math classes.
    Woman: I hate to tell you this, but your major requires four years of math.
    Question: What is the woman telling the man? (12 seconds)

28. Woman: Did you get all the facts you need for that story on the election?
    Man: Yes, and not a moment too soon. We're on the air in 15 minutes.
    Question: Where is this conversation probably taking place? (12 seconds)

29. Man: Would you like to join our debating team?
    Woman: To tell you the truth, I prefer the stage to the podium.
    Question: What will the woman probably do? (12 seconds)

30. Woman: Bob called and said he doesn't want to go bowling with us tonight?
    Man: That's the third time he canceled. What's his problem anyway?
    Question: What does the man want to know? (12 seconds)

This is the end of Part A.

Part B

Directions: In this part, you will hear longer conversations. After each conversation, you will be asked several questions. You will hear the conversations and the questions about them only one time. They will not be repeated. Therefore, you must listen carefully to understand what each speaker says.

After you hear a question, read the four possible answers in your test book and choose which one is the best answer to the question you heard. Then, on your answer sheet, find the number of the question and fill in the space that corresponds to the letter of the answer you have chosen.

Remember, you should not take notes or write on your test paper.

Now let us begin Part B with the first conversation.

Questions 31 through 34. Listen to the conversation between colleagues.
    Man: Hi, Mary, where have you been? I haven't seen you at college in days.
    Woman: My brother and his wife came over from Boston for my parents' 25th wedding anniversary. They're staying with Mom and Dad, but I've been busy taking them here and there to see the sights.
    Man: Twenty-fifth anniversary. That's a golden anniversary, isn't it?
    Woman: No, that's 50 years. Twenty-five is silver, and then there's ruby at forty years, and copper or bronze or something at 15 years.
    Man: I didn't know that. Are all years represented in some way?
    Woman: Sure, even the first year is paper.
    Man: How are you going to celebrate your parents' anniversary? Did you have a party for them yet?
    Woman: No, not yet. We're going to celebrate tonight. We decided to take them out for dinner to a fancy restaurant and then go on to a show. My only problem is that classes start tomorrow and I have lessons to prepare.
    Man: You aren't thinking of doing it all tonight, are you? I wouldn't if I were you.
    Woman: You'll be surprised. I've done it before. I'll just start my lesson plans after everyone has gone to bed.

31. What is the woman's occupation? (12 seconds)

32. According to the conversation, whose anniversary is being celebrated? (12 seconds)

33. According to the conversation, how are they going to celebrate the anniversary? (12 seconds)

34. How does the man feel about Mary doing her lesson plans tonight? (12 seconds)

Questions 35 through 38. Listen to the following conversation between friends.

Woman: Hi, Clark. I thought I'd find you here.
Man: Where else would I be?
Woman: Still hard at work, I see. Do you ever rest?
Man: Not very often. How else am I going to be a famous sculptor?
Woman: But you work 14 hours a day!
Man: That's right. How do you like my latest piece? It's not quite finished yet, of course.
Woman: Not quite? I thought you'd just started it!
Man: Oh, no. I just have to smooth these edges a bit and I'm done. I call it "Lines and Angles."
Woman: Well, it does catch the eye.
Man: Is that all you can say? I've worked on this for weeks! Don't you like it?
Woman: Well, I . . . of course, it's very interesting. And now that I look at it from a distance, it does have a certain appeal.
Man: I knew you'd be crazy about it.
Woman: Yes, well, I'd better go now and let you work. I wouldn't want to disturb a great artist after all!

35. Where is the conversation taking place? (12 seconds)

36. What does the woman imply about the man? (12 seconds)

37. What does the man intend to do? (12 seconds)

38. What does the woman think about the man's new sculpture? (12 seconds)

This is the end of Part B.

Part C

Directions: In this part, you will hear various talks. After each talk, you will be asked several questions. The talks and questions will not be repeated. They will not be written out for you. Therefore, you must listen carefully to understand what the speaker says.

After you hear a question, read the four possible answers in your test book and choose which one is the best answer to the question you heard. Then, on your answer sheet, find the number of the question and fill in the space that corresponds to the letter of the answer you have chosen.

Listen to this sample talk.

You will hear: **The National Health Research Center, perhaps more than any other organization, will directly affect the lives of millions of Americans every day. The Health Research Center volunteers will work all over the United States to provide information on diet and lifestyles. The bulk of the foundation's time will be spent conducting seminars and distributing pamphlets on how to prevent major illness and increase longevity. A free long-distance 800 number is available for anyone with health-related questions.**

Now listen to the following question.

What is the speaker's purpose?

You will read: (A) To get you to join the foundation.
(B) To inform you of the existence of the Health Research Center.
(C) To persuade you to give a donation to the foundation.
(D) To ask you to distribute pamphlets for the foundation.

The best answer to the question, "What is the speaker's purpose?" is *To inform you of the existence of the Health Research Center.* Therefore, you should choose answer (B).

Now listen to the next example.

Why would you use the center's 800 number?

You will read: (A) To volunteer to distribute pamphlets.
(B) To make a contribution to the Health Research Center.
(C) To obtain a schedule of seminars.
(D) To ask questions regarding good health.

The best answer to the question. "Why would you use the center's 800 number?" is *To ask questions regarding good health.* Therefore, you should choose answer (D).

Now let us begin Part C with the first talk.

Questions 39 through 43 refer to the following talk on the planets.

Good afternoon. Today I'd like to continue our study of the planets with a look at Mars. After Venus, Mars is the planet that comes closest to Earth. It is one of the easiest planets to spot in the night sky because of its reddish orange color. We often call it the Red Planet because space probes have shown that the whole planet is a rusty red color. Mars has two tiny moons, called Phobos and Deimos, potato-shaped lumps of rocks pitted with craters. Even the biggest, Phobos, is only about 17 miles across. In some ways, Mars is similar to Earth. Its day is only a little longer than our own. It has seasons. There are ice caps at its north and south poles. And it has an atmosphere in which clouds form and dust storms rage. People once thought that conditions on Mars might be suitable for some forms of life, even for intelligent creatures like humans. But now we know that the Martian climate is too harsh for any form of life as we know it. For most of the time, temperatures are far lower than they are in polar regions on Earth in winter. Also, there is hardly any atmosphere, and it has no oxygen for breathing. However, Mars is the only planet in our solar system that human astronauts could safely land on and explore, as they are expected to by 2010.

39. What is the purpose of this lecture? (12 seconds)

40. In what course was this lecture probably given? (12 seconds)

41. According to the lecture, why is Mars one of the easiest planets to spot in the night sky? (12 seconds)

42. According to the lecture, Mars has all of the following characteristics EXCEPT . . . (12 seconds)

43. The speaker implies that . . . (12 seconds)

Questions 44 through 47.

Good morning, students. I hope you enjoyed our class trip to the Museum of Social History. Did you all have an opportunity to see the exhibition presented by the Food Industry? Following up on that, today's lecture is about chocolate. Our knowledge of the origin of chocolate is rather vague, but we are aware that the Mayans and Aztecs of South America made a drink from the beans of the cacao tree and called it xocoatl. Then, in 1528, this was taken home by the conquering Spanish who named it chocolate. This was the first experience the Europeans had of chocolate, but by the late 1600s, it had spread to most countries in Europe.

In the 18th and 19th centuries, drinking chocolate became a well established activity, but it wasn't until 1847 that Fry and Sons in England introduced "eating chocolate." This remained much of a novelty until Daniel Peter, the famed Swiss chocolatier, was inspired to try to improve its smoothness and taste. Peter's idea was to combine some other ingredient with chocolate to balance its rough flavor. His early experiments with cheese were notoriously unsuccessful and a number of other ill-fated mixtures followed. Finally, in 1874, Peter stumbled on the perfect answer: milk.

Nowadays milk chocolate is made of at least 10 percent chocolate mass, or raw chocolate, and 12 percent milk solids combined with sugar, cocoa butter, and vanilla. It is also the type of chocolate most often chosen by children because it is less bitter than the dark varieties.

44. What is the main topic of the lecture? (12 seconds)

45. Which part of the world did chocolate originally come from? (12 seconds)

46. Daniel Peter was NOT successful in his attempt to . . . (12 seconds)

47. According to the lecture, why do children like milk chocolate better than dark chocolate? (12 seconds)

Questions 48 through 50.

May I have your attention, please. Anyone waiting to go on the Universal Studios tour should join the line beside the kiosk, near the shops. The next tour will be leaving in 5 minutes so don't delay. Places visited will include the back lot where much of the filming takes place. You will also have the chance to imagine what it would be like to be attacked by a killer shark or caught up in a battle between the galaxies. When visiting the Special Effects Studio, some of the magic tricks of the film trade will be revealed to you. If you'd like to appear in a movie with a famous movie star, look out for the Screen Test Comedy Theater. For the children, there is a new game where they can search for props and win some very special prizes. In the Entertainment Center, there is an explosive live show and Hollywood's most daring stuntmen will perform death defying acts in the Stunt Show. Finally, after seeing animals perform incredible tricks at the Animal Actors Stage, the tour will finish at the restaurant where you can refresh yourselves, in the style of the 1880s, after all the excitement of the tour.

48. What is the purpose of this announcement? (12 seconds)

49. According to the announcement, where should you wait to join the Universal Studios tour? (12 seconds)

50. What is the speaker's tone? (12 seconds)

Stop work on Section 1.

Practice Test 5

LISTENING COMPREHENSION

In this section of the test, you will have an opportunity to demonstrate your ability to understand conversations and talks in English. In this section, there are answers to all the questions based on the information heard.

Part A

Directions: In Part A, you will hear short conversations between two people. At the end of each conversation, you will hear a question about the conversation. The conversation and question will not be repeated. Therefore, you must listen carefully to understand what each speaker says. After you hear a question, read the four possible answers in your test book and choose the best answer to the question you heard. Then, on your answer sheet, find the number of the question and fill in the space that corresponds to the letter of the answer you have chosen.

Listen to an example on the recording:

      Man: **What seems to be the problem, ma'am?**
      Woman: **Well, the light switch is broken and a plug needs repairing.**
      Question: **What kind of work does the man probably do?**

In your book you will read: (A) He's a carpenter.
                              (B) He's a plumber.
                              (C) He's an electrician.
                              (D) He's an engineer.

From the conversation, you learn that the light switch is broken and a plug needs repairing. The best answer to the question, "What kind of work does the man probably do?" is *He's an electrician*. Therefore, the correct choice is (C).

Now go on to the first question.

1.   Man: Two for lunch. We don't have a reservation.
      Woman: There will be a thirty-minute wait.
      Question: Where does this conversation take place? (12 seconds)

2.   Woman: Where can we meet to discuss our assignment?
      Man: What about the snack bar at noon?
      Question: What is the man suggesting? (12 seconds)

3.   Man: How can I get the number of this college in Texas?
      Woman: I'm not sure. Let's ask information.
      Question: What does the woman mean? (12 seconds)

4. Woman: Shall we go to a play or a movie?
    Man: It's all the same to me.
    Question: What does the man mean? (12 seconds)

5. Woman: Would you like to study with us in the library?
    Man: I'd rather study at home.
    Question: What will the man probably do? (12 seconds)

6. Woman: John, will you type that paper for Nancy?
    Man: I'll have Peter do it on his computer in the office.
    Question: Who will type the paper? (12 seconds)

7. Man: How long has Susan been in this country – a year?
    Woman: At least, if not longer.
    Question: What is the woman saying about Susan? (12 seconds)

8. Woman: What about getting two seats in the front row?
    Man: Sounds good to me.
    Question: What does the man mean? (12 seconds)

9. Man: That's a good song he's playing, isn't it?
    Woman: I wish he'd lower the volume
    Question: What is the woman's opinion? (12 seconds)

10. Woman: The American custom of using first names is so difficult for me.
    Man: I don't call my professors by their first names.
    Question: What does the woman mean? (12 seconds)

11. Man: What about bringing John along to the meeting?
    Woman: That isn't such a bad idea.
    Question: What does the woman mean? (12 seconds)

12. Woman: I thought that lecture was excellent.
    Man: Well, I've heard better.
    Question: What does the man mean? (12 seconds)

13. Man: Should we go to the presentation in the auditorium tonight?
    Woman: Only if we have to.
    Question: What does the woman mean? (12 seconds)

14. Man: Do you need a ride to the airport on Monday?
    Woman: Jim promised to take me on his way to work.
    Question: What does the woman mean? (12 seconds)

15. Woman: Have you finished your term paper yet?
    Man: I started to read a novel instead.
    Question: What does the man imply? (12 seconds)

16. Man: I don't see why we have to paint flowers. I'd much rather do a landscape.
    Woman: I don't mind. I think it's important for us to do a variety of work.
    Question: What are these people probably doing? (12 seconds)

17. Man: Did you have a good time on your vacation?
    Woman: Yes, but I could have done without the castles and museums.
    Question: What can be inferred from this woman's statement? (12 seconds)

18. Man: I guess Martin isn't coming to the party.
    Woman: Oh, don't worry. He'll show up eventually.
    Question: What does the woman say about Martin? (12 seconds)

19. Woman: Are you going to enter the ski jumping competition today?
    Man: No, I've done that once too many times, which is why I'm limping.
    Question: What does the man imply? (12 seconds)

20. Man: What a great day for a picnic. I've even brought some potato salad.
    Woman: So, you made it after all!
    Question: What had the woman assumed about the man? (12 seconds)

21. Man: Wasn't it a great weekend? I stayed in and read a book I've been wanting to get
               to for a long time.
    Woman: Well, you may have liked the rain, but I had outdoor plans.
    Question: What does the woman mean? (12 seconds)

22. Woman: Would you like me to get you a placard for handicapped parking?
    Man: No, thank you, Doctor. Save that for the truly disabled.
    Question: What is the woman offering? (12 seconds)

23. Woman: What did your parents do when they saw your grades?
    Man: Just as I predicted, they went through the roof.
    Question: What is the man saying about his parents? (12 seconds)

24. Man: It's taken me a week just to find the books I need to write my term paper on
               genetic engineering.
    Woman: You should have talked to me about it. I had to do some research on that subject
               last semester.
    Question: What is the woman implying? (12 seconds)

25. Woman: I saw Jeremy in biology lab today.
    Man: Oh, so he didn't drop out after all.
    Question: What did the man assume? (12 seconds)

26. Man: What do you think?
    Woman: I'm afraid we have quite a bit of work to do on that mouth, at least two fillings
               and maybe one extraction.
    Question: What is the woman's probable occupation? (12 seconds)

27. Man: It's Thursday already and I still don't have a date to the dance. I just don't know
               whom to ask.
    Woman: How about my cousin?
    Question: What is the woman suggesting? (12 seconds)

28. Woman: I have to run to my English literature class, but I still have all these test tubes and
               beakers to put away.

154

Man: Don't worry. I'll take care of everything of you.
Question: What is the man offering to do for the woman? (12 seconds)

29. Woman: What happened last night? I thought you were going to propose to Elaine?
    Man: It's very simple. I got cold feet.
    Question: What does the man mean? (12 seconds)

30. Man: Patsy, I thought we were going to the museum today. You know how I've been looking forward to it.
    Woman: But, Sean, it's such a beautiful day that I'd rather go to the botanical gardens.
    Question: What can be inferred from this conversation? (12 seconds)

This is the end of Part A.

Part B

Directions: In this part, you will hear longer conversations. After each conversation, you will be asked several questions. You will hear the conversations and the questions about them only one time. They will not be repeated. Therefore, you must listen carefully to understand what each speaker says.

After you hear a question, read the four possible answers in your test book and choose which one is the best answer to the question you heard. Then, on your answer sheet, find the number of the question and fill in the space that corresponds to the letter of the answer you have chosen.

Remember, you should not take notes or write on your test paper.

Now let us begin Part B with the first conversation.

Questions 31 through 33 are based on the following conversation between two students.
    Woman: What topic did you finally choose for the term paper for your World Economics class?
    Man: After tossing around a few ideas, I finally settled on the difference between Japanese and American styles of management.
    Woman: Hmm. Why did you choose a topic like that?
    Man: Well, I'm planning to study Business in graduate school next year. After that, I hope to start my own company.
    Woman: Isn't that a coincidence! I'm doing a paper on how Japanese management styles are being adapted by American firms for my Comparative Cultures class.
    Man: Why don't we sit down and share some of our sources after we've each been to the library?
    Woman: Great idea! Should we meet at the snack bar next Wednesday at this time?
    Man: That's fine with me. See you then.

31. What are the speakers mostly discussing? (12 seconds)

32. What do the speakers have in common? (12 seconds)

33. According to the conversation, what will the man and woman do next Wednesday? (12 seconds)

Questions 34 through 38 are based on a business conversation.
    Man: How can I help you?
    Woman: I'd like to open a new savings account, please.
    Man: You'll need to deposit $100 to open your account.
    Woman: But I called last week and was told it was $50.

Man:	I'm sorry, but we've changed our policy.
Woman:	You mean that if I'd come last week, I could have opened an account and today I can't!
Man:	That's right. I'm very sorry.
Woman:	I want to see the person in charge.
Man:	You're speaking to him.
Woman:	In that case, I guess I'll have to go someplace else with my business.
Man:	Now don't be hasty. Maybe we can work something out. After all, every person who walks in here is a valued customer. Tell me, are you a student by any chance?
Woman:	Yes, I'm enrolled at the university.
Man:	Why didn't you say that before! There's no problem then. Our minimum amount for opening a student account is $50.
Woman:	Well, that's just fine, but now I don't know if I want to open an account here.
Man:	We'll give you a free backpack. It's perfect for carrying your books.
Woman:	Where are the forms?

34. Where is the conversation taking place? (12 seconds)

35. Who are the two speakers? (12 seconds)

36. According to the conversation, what kind of account does the woman want to open? (12 seconds)

37. How does the woman feel about the new $100 policy? (12 seconds)

38. What will the woman probably do? (12 seconds)

This is the end of Part B.

Part C

Directions: In this part, you will hear various talks. After each talk, you will be asked several questions. The talks and questions will not be repeated. They will not be written out for you. Therefore, you must listen carefully to understand what the speaker says.

After you hear a question, read the four possible answers in your test book and choose which one is the best answer to the question you heard. Then, on your answer sheet, find the number of the question and fill in the space that corresponds to the letter of the answer you have chosen.

Listen to this sample talk.
You will hear: **The National Health Research Center, perhaps more than any other organization, will directly affect the lives of millions of Americans every day. The Health Research Center volunteers will work all over the United States to provide information on diet and lifestyles. The bulk of the foundation's time will be spent conducting seminars and distributing pamphlets on how to prevent major illness and increase longevity. A free long-distance 800 number is available for anyone with health-related questions.**

Now listen to the following question.

What is the speaker's purpose?

You will read: (A)   To get you to join the foundation.
(B)   To inform you of the existence of the Health Research Center.
(C)   To persuade you to give a donation to the foundation.
(D)   To ask you to distribute pamphlets for the foundation.

The best answer to the question, "What is the speaker's purpose?" is *To inform you of the existence of the Health Research Center.* Therefore, you should choose answer (B).

Now listen to the next example.

Why would you use the center's 800 number?

You will read: (A)   To volunteer to distribute pamphlets.
(B)   To make a contribution to the Health Research Center.
(C)   To obtain a schedule of seminars.
(D)   To ask questions regarding good health.

The best answer to the question. "Why would you use the center's 800 number?" is *To ask questions regarding good health.* Therefore, you should choose answer (D).

Now let us begin Part C with the first talk.

Questions 39 through 43.

Ladies and gentleman, why don't you gather round here. I'll demonstrate to you our new and useful fire or security alarm radio transmitter. As you all know, in an emergency such as a fire, accident, or crime in the home, your safety depends upon how quickly you can contact emergency services. A vital part of the message you give to the fire, ambulance, or police department is the exact location of the emergency. Crucial time can be lost giving addresses and working out the best route. That's where our radio transmitter attached to your fire or security alarm can save your life. In an emergency, it automatically transmits details of the location in seconds. This is something no one should live without. And today only, they're on sale for 25 percent off their original price. Think about it. Your family's safety is at stake.

39.   What is the main idea of this talk? (12 seconds)

40.   What is the purpose of this talk? (12 seconds)

41.   What is the speaker's probable occupation? (12 seconds)

42.   According to the talk, what does safety in an emergency depend upon? (12 seconds)

43.   According to the talk, what does the alarm radio transmitter do? (12 seconds)

Questions 44 through 47.

I would like to greet you all and tell you how happy we are here at the Admissions Office to have you at Glenville College's annual welcome meeting for international students. A representative from the Registrar's Office will be here later to answer any questions you might have regarding registration procedures. We are also very happy to have with us the

International Student Advisor, who will speak to you about your special concerns today. He also conducts weekly question and answer sessions to help you with your future plans.

44. Who is the speaker? (12 seconds)

45. According to the talk, who will discuss special concerns? (12 seconds)

46. What does the speaker say about registration questions? (12 seconds)

47. How often does the college have these welcome sessions? (12 seconds)

Questions 48 through 50.
Thank you for joining us today. I hope you all enjoyed our new entomology exhibit. Before you leave, I'd like to give a brief talk on insect behavior. I'll start by answering one of your questions, which was how can an insect walk on walls and ceilings.

Well, as you know, an insect such as a fly or beetle walks on six legs. It supports itself on three legs while it moves the other three legs forward. Then it switches legs and supports itself on the other three. Many insects can walk on walls and ceilings because most of those surfaces are quite rough. They just hold onto the tiny rough projections on the surface by means of claws at the end of their limbs. Other insects hold onto smooth surfaces by means of an adhesive organ called the pulvillus. This often takes the form of a hair-covered cushion located on an insect's foot. The hairs have soft, flattened ends, and when they press against a smooth surface, an adhesion takes place. So that is how they manage to crawl over walls and ceilings.

48. What is the main topic of the talk? (12 seconds)

49. Where was this lecture probably given? (12 seconds)

50. According to the talk, how do insects crawl over walls and ceilings? (12 seconds)

Stop work on Section 1.

Answer Keys
Practice Test 1
Section 1

1	C	11	D	21	C	31	B	41	A
2	C	12	C	22	D	32	A	42	C
3	B	13	D	23	B	33	D	43	B
4	B	14	C	24	B	34	C	44	D
5	D	15	B	25	A	35	B	45	A
6	B	16	A	26	D	36	D	46	A
7	C	17	D	27	C	37	A	47	B
8	C	18	B	28	A	38	D	48	B
9	D	19	B	29	B	39	C	49	D
10	D	20	C	30	D	40	B	50	C

Section 2

1	B	11	A	21	B	31	A
2	C	12	C	22	D	32	A
3	D	13	B	23	C	33	B
4	A	14	C	24	D	34	A
5	D	15	A	25	B	35	A
6	A	16	B	26	B	36	A
7	B	17	C	27	A	37	C
8	C	18	D	28	D	38	A
9	A	19	D	29	C	39	B
10	D	20	C	30	C	40	B

Section 3

1	B	11	A	21	C	31	B	41	C
2	C	12	C	22	D	32	A	42	C
3	C	13	B	23	C	33	D	43	D
4	B	14	B	24	D	34	C	44	D
5	D	15	C	25	B	35	D	45	C
6	C	16	B	26	B	36	A	46	B
7	D	17	A	27	C	37	B	47	A
8	B	18	D	28	B	38	D	48	B
9	A	19	B	29	A	39	B	49	C
10	D	20	D	30	A	40	B	50	D

Practice Test 2

Section 1

1	D	11	A	21	B	31	B	41	A
2	C	12	C	22	C	32	D	42	B
3	B	13	C	23	C	33	A	43	D
4	C	14	D	24	A	34	C	44	C
5	D	15	D	25	B	35	B	45	C
6	A	16	D	26	D	36	C	46	B
7	A	17	B	27	D	37	D	47	B
8	C	18	D	28	A	38	B	48	A
9	B	19	A	29	B	39	D	49	C
10	D	20	B	30	D	40	C	50	D

Section 2

1	B	11	B	21	B	31	B
2	C	12	C	22	C	32	C
3	A	13	D	23	B	33	D
4	D	14	A	24	B	34	A
5	B	15	B	25	A	35	B
6	D	16	A	26	C	36	A
7	A	17	A	27	D	37	D
8	D	18	D	28	C	38	B
9	C	19	D	29	C	39	B
10	A	20	C	30	D	40	A

Section 3

1	C	11	D	21	B	31	B	41	A
2	A	12	D	22	C	32	B	42	C
3	B	13	B	23	D	33	C	43	D
4	C	14	C	24	B	34	D	44	D
5	D	15	C	25	A	35	C	45	C
6	D	16	B	26	D	36	C	46	B
7	B	17	B	27	A	37	A	47	D
8	D	18	C	28	D	38	D	48	C
9	A	19	A	29	A	39	D	49	D
10	C	20	D	30	D	40	B	50	D

160

Practice Test 3

Section 1

1	B	11	C	21	A	31	C	41	D
2	D	12	C	22	B	32	D	42	B
3	C	13	A	23	A	33	C	43	C
4	A	14	B	24	C	34	C	44	D
5	B	15	C	25	B	35	A	45	B
6	A	16	A	26	D	36	C	46	B
7	B	17	C	27	C	37	B	47	D
8	D	18	B	28	A	38	D	48	C
9	B	19	B	29	C	39	C	49	D
10	A	20	D	30	D	40	D	50	B

Section 2

1	B	11	C	21	C	31	D
2	C	12	B	22	A	32	D
3	D	13	D	23	C	33	A
4	A	14	A	24	A	34	C
5	B	15	C	25	C	35	B
6	C	16	D	26	D	36	B
7	A	17	B	27	B	37	B
8	C	18	B	28	A	38	B
9	A	19	B	29	C	39	B
10	C	20	B	30	A	40	B

Section 3

1	B	11	D	21	C	31	A	41	A
2	A	12	D	22	D	32	B	42	B
3	C	13	B	23	B	33	C	43	A
4	B	14	D	24	D	34	C	44	D
5	D	15	B	25	A	35	B	45	B
6	B	16	C	26	B	36	D	46	D
7	A	17	D	27	A	37	A	47	D
8	C	18	A	28	C	38	D	48	C
9	C	19	B	29	A	39	B	49	D
10	B	20	A	30	D	40	C	50	D

Practice Test 4
Section 1

1	C	11	B	21	C	31	C	41	A
2	C	12	C	22	A	32	B	42	D
3	D	13	B	23	A	33	A	43	C
4	C	14	B	24	B	34	B	44	C
5	B	15	B	25	B	35	D	45	B
6	A	16	B	26	D	36	B	46	C
7	B	17	D	27	D	37	A	47	A
8	B	18	A	28	C	38	C	48	C
9	C	19	D	29	B	39	A	49	C
10	D	20	C	30	A	40	B	50	A

Section 2

1	D	11	A	21	D	31	C
2	A	12	D	22	C	32	D
3	B	13	B	23	C	33	B
4	C	14	C	24	A	34	C
5	A	15	B	25	C	35	D
6	A	16	A	26	C	36	D
7	B	17	A	27	B	37	D
8	D	18	A	28	D	38	A
9	B	19	B	29	B	39	C
10	B	20	D	30	B	40	C

Section 3

1	A	11	B	21	D	31	D	41	C
2	D	12	C	22	A	32	B	42	D
3	C	13	D	23	D	33	C	43	B
4	B	14	B	24	C	34	A	44	A
5	C	15	C	25	B	35	C	45	A
6	B	16	B	26	A	36	D	46	A
7	C	17	A	27	C	37	D	47	C
8	C	18	B	28	C	38	A	48	C
9	A	19	C	29	B	39	B	49	A
10	D	20	D	30	D	40	B	50	B

Practice Test 5

Section 1

1	A	11	C	21	D	31	C	41	D
2	B	12	A	22	C	32	D	42	C
3	C	13	B	23	C	33	C	43	A
4	D	14	D	24	B	34	C	44	A
5	D	15	D	25	D	35	A	45	B
6	A	16	C	26	A	36	D	46	C
7	B	17	C	27	A	37	A	47	D
8	C	18	A	28	C	38	B	48	C
9	A	19	A	29	B	39	C	49	D
10	A	20	A	30	D	40	B	50	B

Section 2

1	B	11	A	21	D	31	D
2	A	12	C	22	B	32	B
3	C	13	A	23	D	33	D
4	D	14	D	24	A	34	A
5	B	15	B	25	D	35	B
6	D	16	C	26	B	36	D
7	A	17	C	27	C	37	C
8	D	18	D	28	B	38	A
9	C	19	A	29	B	39	A
10	B	20	C	30	D	40	C

Section 3

1	B	11	B	21	B	31	C	41	C
2	B	12	C	22	B	32	D	42	C
3	V	13	B	23	D	33	D	43	A
4	S	14	C	24	B	34	B	44	B
5	B	15	C	25	B	35	D	45	D
6	D	16	A	26	A	36	C	46	B
7	A	17	A	27	D	37	C	47	A
8	B	18	D	28	C	38	C	48	C
9	D	19	B	29	A	39	C	49	C
10	C	20	B	30	C	40	B	50	A